COBOL from BASIC
A short self-instructional

Michael Oatey
Lecturer, Distance Learning Unit

and Carl Payne
Principal Lecturer in Computing

South Bank Polytechnic, London

Pitman

PITMAN PUBLISHING LIMITED
128 Long Acre, London WC2E 9AN

A Longman Group Company

© M Oatey and C Payne 1986

First published in Great Britain 1986

British Library Cataloguing in Publication Data

Oatey, Michael
COBOL from BASIC — A short self-instructional course.
1. COBOL (Computer program language).
I. Title   II. Payne, Carl.
005.13'3   QA76.73.C25
ISBN 0 273 02495 7

All rights reserved. No part of this publication may be reproduced, stored in a retrieval system, or transmitted, in any form or by any means, electronic, mechanical, photocopying, recording and/or otherwise without the prior written permission of the publishers. This book may not be lent, resold, hired out or otherwise disposed of by way of trade in any form of binding, or cover other than that in which it is published, without the prior consent of the publishers.

Printed at The Bath Press, Avon

Contents

How to use this book   1
Introduction   2

Unit 1   Some simple statements   4

Unit 2   Further statements   18

Unit 3   Text and screen displays   30
Exercise A   40

Unit 4   Field descriptions   42

Unit 5   Record descriptions   52

Unit 6   Sequential files   64
Exercise B   76

Unit 7   Indexed files   78
Exercise C   91

Unit 8   Further topics   94
Exercise D   104

Postscript   80

Appendix   1 Layout of a COBOL program   109
2 Running a COBOL program   110

Answers to Further Questions and Exercises   114

Index   124

Acknowledgements

The authors would like to thank colleagues and students who have commented on, or worked through, drafts of this book, in particular: Terry Baylis, Mary Emmanuel, Dick Merrall and Angela Roberts.

Michael Oatey would also like to acknowledge comments on earlier self-instructional material on COBOL from colleagues at the Sperry Univac training centre (UK), where he worked from 1977 to 1979.

How to use this book

The book contains eight main Units. Questions are interspersed within the text of each Unit. These questions are preceded by the symbol ◐, for example the following question appears on page 18 in Unit 2:

◐ Qu 2.1 Write a sequence that will display the result of adding together three numbers typed in by the user. Use data-names D, E, F and SUM.

Answers are given at the bottom of the next page but one, so the answer to the above question appears at the bottom of page 20.
   Always write down your answers before checking them. If you get an incorrect answer, re-read the preceding text and try to see where you went wrong.
   Further questions are given at the end of each Unit. Answers to these questions are at the back of the book.
   From time to time longer Exercises are included, which consolidate material in previous Units. Answers to the Exercises are at the back of the book.

Introduction

COBOL stands for COmmon Business Oriented Language. It is the most widely used language for commercial and business applications on larger computers, and is becoming increasingly available on microcomputers.

This book is oriented to COBOL on microcomputers in general, and to a version called CIS COBOL in particular (CIS stands for Compact, Interactive and Standard). All programs will run in CIS COBOL and LEVEL II COBOL (both produced by Micro Focus Ltd). However, variations in other COBOL versions are indicated (and summarized on page 113).

The purpose of this book is to introduce the facilities of COBOL, particularly screen input–output and file handling. Program design is not discussed in detail, although structured techniques are used. By the end of the book you should be able to write useful programs using sequential and random files.

Previous knowledge

The book assumes you have at least an elementary knowledge of BASIC and that you have run some simple programs. However, readers with a working knowledge of languages such as Pascal and FORTRAN should have no difficulty, even if some of the references to BASIC are not fully appreciated.

The level of BASIC assumed is that you can write simple programs using numeric variables (e.g. A and B) and string variables (e.g. A$ and B$) and the following statements:

Statement type	Examples in BASIC
output	PRINT A
	PRINT "GAS UNITS = ", U
assignment	LET A = B / C
	LET A$ = "16 HIGH ST."
branching	GOTO 10
input	INPUT A$
decision	IF A$ = "YES" THEN C = C + 1
	IF A < 0 THEN PRINT "ERROR"

A knowledge of READ and DATA statements would also be useful, but is not essential.

This level of BASIC is reached in the companion volume *BASIC: A short self-instructional course* (see the back cover for details).

Running programs

Before you can start running most programs in COBOL, you have to learn rather more than you do in BASIC. In the main text of this book, the first complete program you can run is not given until Unit 4 (page 45). This is not a serious drawback since it is assumed that you have run some BASIC programs and so are familiar with entering programs and with screen displays. Further, the book can be used by those who want an interactive course but have limited or no access to a computer that supports COBOL (though of course the serious student must run programs sooner or later).

However, if you do want to run a program before Unit 4, you can try the short demonstration program given in Appendix 2 (p. 110). You should preferably reach the end of Unit 1 before running this program.

Unit 1 Some simple statements

A COBOL program consists of up to four divisions. The first division we will look at, the Procedure Division, contains statements similar in action to statements in BASIC. However, note that the Procedure Division examples given in Unit 1 form only part of a program and cannot be run by themselves. (If you would like to see a complete program with all four divisions now, turn to Appendix 2, page 110 for a short example or to page 77 for a longer example.)

Here is a complete Procedure Division from a program that multiplies two numbers together:

```
PROCEDURE DIVISION.
    MULTIPLY 22 BY 4 GIVING A.
    DISPLAY A.
    STOP RUN.
```

The above Procedure Division contains three statements: a MULTIPLY, a DISPLAY, and a STOP RUN statement. The MULTIPLY statement multiplies 22 by 4 and places the result in a variable called A. The DISPLAY statement displays the value of A (that is, 88) on a video screen. The STOP RUN statement shows the end of the program has been reached.

Below is another Procedure Division, this time containing a SUBTRACT statement:

```
PROCEDURE DIVISION.
    SUBTRACT 4 FROM 22 GIVING B.
    DISPLAY B.
    STOP RUN.
```

full stops

Notice that each line ends with a full stop. A full stop must be placed after a division heading and at the end of a division, but full stops can be optional after statements. However, use of full stops is a common source of error and it is a good habit to include full stops even when they are optional. The indentation of statements under the division heading by four spaces is also significant.

Full details of the format of COBOL programs will be given later. For the present we will end all division headings and statements with a full stop, and will indent all statements by four spaces.

◐ **Qu 1.1** When a program containing the last Procedure Division above is executed, what is displayed on the screen? (Remember that answers to interspersed questions are at the bottom of the next page but one.)

◐ **Qu 1.2** Write a complete Procedure Division that will multiply 175 by 0.33 and display the result on the screen. Use a variable called C.

The following statements show simplified general forms of arithmetic statements, using variables called X, Y and Z:

    ADD X, Y GIVING Z.
    SUBTRACT X FROM Y GIVING Z.
    MULTIPLY X BY Y GIVING Z.
    DIVIDE X INTO Y GIVING Z.

The variables X and Y can be replaced by numbers.

Notice that the form of the ADD statement is different from the others in that there is no word (such as AND) between X and Y. The comma is included for readability only and can be omitted. All commas (and semicolons) are used only for readability in COBOL and are always optional, but in this book we will include commas when they are permitted.

◐ **Qu 1.3** Write two COBOL statements equivalent to the following in BASIC (or in ordinary maths):
    A = B + C
    D = A / E

COBOL allows more meaningful names for variables than just letters like A or B (as do some versions of BASIC). Names should be chosen to make a program as readable as possible. For example, if we use the following variable names in a program on test scores:

> MARKS1 for marks in the first test
> MARKS2 for marks in the second test
> MARKS3 for marks in the third test
> TOTAL   for total marks

then this statement can be readily followed:

> ADD MARKS1, MARKS2, MARKS3 GIVING TOTAL.

This statement also shows that several values can be added together in an ADD statement.

◐ **Qu 1.4** Write a statement that calculates distance travelled (use the variable DIST) given the initial mileage (use the variable STARTMILES) and the final mileage (use the variable ENDMILES).

We now move on from arithmetic statements to DISPLAY and STOP RUN statements, which were also included in the Procedure Division examples given earlier.

The DISPLAY statement is used to display values and results on a video screen. For example, to display the value of TOTAL we write:

> DISPLAY TOTAL.

or to display all test marks on one line of the screen, we write:

> DISPLAY MARKS1, MARKS2, MARKS3.

The spacing of the output on the screen will be considered later. (Again, the commas are optional in the DISPLAY statement.)

The DISPLAY statement is similar to the PRINT statement in BASIC. However, unlike the PRINT statement, the DISPLAY statement cannot be used for calculations. (For example, MARKS1, MARKS2 and MARKS3 cannot be added together in the DISPLAY statement.)

Finally we come to the STOP RUN statement. The last statement executed in a Procedure Division is always STOP RUN in this book.

◐ Qu 1.5 Write a complete Procedure Division that first calculates the tax on an item of a given price, assuming a tax rate of 15% (multiply by 0.15); then calculates the total charge including tax; and then displays the price, tax and charge on one line of the screen. Use variables named PRICE, TAX and CHARGE.

Before continuing, a point of terminology needs to be explained. Up to now we have been talking about *variables*, which is a term used in BASIC. However, items that have been called variables are more usually called *fields* in COBOL, for reasons given later. So in the Procedure Division you wrote for Qu 1.5 above, you used three fields (named PRICE, TAX and CHARGE). In future we will use the term field rather than variable.

Ans 1.1   18

Ans 1.2   PROCEDURE DIVISION.
              MULTIPLY 175 BY 0.33 GIVING C.
              DISPLAY C.
              STOP RUN.
Did you remember the full stops?

Ans 1.3   ADD B, C GIVING A.
              DIVIDE E INTO A GIVING D.

MOVE statements

Another common statement in the Procedure Division is the MOVE statement. This is used for assigning values, for example:

>   MOVE 15 TO B.
>   MOVE 0.25 TO RATE.
>   MOVE 7 TO EGGS.

In ordinary maths (and in BASIC) these examples might be written as: B = 15, RATE = 0.25, and EGGS = 7. Or in English we could say: assign the value of 15 to B, make the rate equal to 0.25, and set the price of eggs to 7.

Qu 1.6 Write MOVE statements to achieve the following:
(a) assign to BONUS the value of 150
(b) give B the value 2.5
(c) C = 24

Now consider the following statement:

>   MOVE A TO B.

This of course means move or assign the value of A to B. So if A has the value 9, then B is given the value 9 after execution of the statement. In such a statement, A is called the *sending* field and B the *receiving* field for obvious reasons. The receiving field is changed to the new value, but the sending field remains unchanged. So if before the statement is executed A is 9 and B is 5, then after execution A is 9 and B is 9. The original value of B is lost.

Ans 1.4   SUBTRACT STARTMILES FROM ENDMILES GIVING DIST.

It can be useful to think of fields (like variables in BASIC) as physical locations in the computer's store or memory:

A □
B □

locations in the computer's store

Before the MOVE statement, the contents of these fields are 9 and 5:

A |9|
B |5|

After the MOVE statement, the contents of field A are placed in field B. The original contents of B are overwritten:

A |9|
B |$\cancel{5}$9|

Similarly, arithmetic statements have sending and receiving fields. For example in:

MULTIPLY X BY Y GIVING Z.

X and Y are sending fields (which remain unchanged), while Z is a receiving field (which is changed). If before execution X is 5, Y is 6, and Z is 7, then afterwards X is 5, Y is 6, and Z is 30.

Ans 1.5   PROCEDURE DIVISION.
              MULTIPLY PRICE BY 0.15 GIVING TAX.
              ADD PRICE, TAX GIVING CHARGE.
              DISPLAY PRICE, TAX, CHARGE.
              STOP RUN.

◐ Qu 1.7 The figures in brackets after each statement below show field values before execution of the statement. Give field values after execution of each statement.

      (a) MOVE E TO F.   (E = 0, F = 55)
      (b) MOVE 0.3 TO RATE.   (RATE = 0.2)
      (c) ADD X, Y GIVING Z.   (X = 17, Y = 5, Z = 25)

A MOVE statement can have more than one receiving field. For example, the following statement has four receiving fields:

      MOVE A TO B, C, D, E.

If A has the value 70, then after execution B, C, D and E will also have the value 70. (Again, commas are optional.)

Similarly, an ADD statement can have more than two sending fields (that is, it can add more than two numbers together as we noted earlier). The following Procedure Division contains a MOVE statement with two receiving fields and an ADD statement with three sending fields:

```
PROCEDURE DIVISION.
    MOVE 50 TO MARKS1, MARKS2.
    MOVE 20 TO MARKS3.
    ADD MARKS1, MARKS2, MARKS3 GIVING TOTAL.
    DIVIDE 3 INTO TOTAL GIVING AVERAGE.
    DISPLAY AVERAGE.
    STOP RUN.
```

◐ Qu 1.8 What value is displayed on the screen when a program containing the above Procedure Division is run?

◐ Qu 1.9 Rewrite the following in a shorter form:
      MOVE 999 TO A.
      MOVE 999 TO B.
      MOVE 999 TO C.

Ans 1.6 (a) MOVE 150 TO BONUS.
        (b) MOVE 2.5 TO B.
        (c) MOVE 24 TO C.

Data-names, literals and general formats

We have seen that a field may be thought of as a physical location in the computer's memory, and that a field can be given a meaningful name such as MARKS1 or TOTAL. In COBOL, names given to fields are called a *data-names*.

Rules for making up data-names are listed below (although you do not need to remember them at this stage):

1 Only letters, digits and hyphens can be used (so no spaces are allowed)
2 Hyphens may not appear at the beginning or end
3 At least one character must be a letter
4 The length must not exceed 30 characters
5 COBOL *reserved words* must not be used

Reserved words (rule 5) are key words used by the language itself, such as SUBTRACT, FROM, MOVE and TO. Most comprehensive books or manuals on COBOL give a complete list of reserved words.

Note that spaces cannot be used in data-names, but hyphens can be used (rule 1). Hyphens are very useful for making data-names more readable (for example, DISCOUNT-RATE is better than DISCOUNTRATE) and we shall use them where appropriate from now on.

◐ Qu 1.10 Identify any errors in the following data-names: (a) TOTAL-MARKS, (b) ADD, (c) PART- , (d) GROSS PAY, (e) 123A, (f) 1–23, (g) STOCK-PART-IDENTIFICATION-NUMBER, (h) PAY-£.

We have looked at two types of element in statements: data-names (such as TOTAL-MARKS) and reserved words (such as ADD). The third, and last, element type in statements is the *literal*. Literals are elements in statements that are interpreted 'literally' by the computer, such as numbers. So in the statement:

MULTIPLY 3.5 BY 12 GIVING RESULT.

the numbers 3.5 and 12 are literals (while RESULT is a data-name and MULTIPLY, BY and GIVING are reserved words). There are different types of literals but, for the moment, assume a literal in the general formats given below means a number.

Now consider this statement:

    MOVE 33.3 TO NUM-1, NUM-2.

◐ **Qu 1.11** In the above statement, classify each element as a data-name, literal or reserved word.

General formats General formats for statements are very useful for reference and as memory joggers. COBOL has well established conventions for showing general formats. Here are examples for the MULTIPLY and MOVE statements:

MULTIPLY $\begin{Bmatrix} \text{data-name-1} \\ \text{literal-1} \end{Bmatrix}$ BY $\begin{Bmatrix} \text{data-name-2} \\ \text{literal-2} \end{Bmatrix}$ GIVING data-name-3

MOVE $\begin{Bmatrix} \text{data-name-1} \\ \text{literal-1} \end{Bmatrix}$ TO data-name-2 . . .

We will now use these examples, together with the general format shown on page 52, to illustrate the rules for interpreting general formats. The rules are:

- upper case words underlined are mandatory (e.g. MULTIPLY and TO)

- upper case words not underlined are optional (e.g. IS on page 62)

- lower case words show elements supplied by the programmer (e.g. data-name-1 and literal)

- curley brackets (or braces) show a mandatory choice (e.g. data-name-1 or literal-1)

Ans 1.7   (a) $E = 0, F = 0$ (b) $RATE = 0.3$ (c) $X = 17, Y = 5, Z = 22$

Ans 1.8   40

Ans 1.9   MOVE 999 TO A, B, C.

− square brackets show optional elements (e.g. VALUE IS literal on page 62)

− an ellipsis (. . .) shows optional repetition of the preceding element(s) (e.g. after data-name-2 in the MOVE statement there can be data-name-3, data-name-4 and so on, this is any number of receiving fields)

◐ Qu 1.12   Using the above general formats for the MULTIPLY and MOVE statements as a guide, correct any errors in the following statements:
        (a) MULTIPLY 3, 12 GIVING RESULT.
        (b) MULTIPLY 3 BY NUM-1 GIVING NUM-2.
        (c) MULTIPLY NUM-1 BY NUM-2 BY NUM-3 GIVING RESULT.
        (d) MOVE NUM TO 3.

Ans 1.10   (b) reserved word   (c) hyphen at the end   (d) contains a space   (f) contains no letter   (g) exceeds 30 characters   (h) contains a character other than a letter, digit or hyphen

Below are given general formats for statements introduced in this Unit. Most of the formats are simplified in that extra elements may be added (for example, all arithmetic statements can include a ROUNDED option to round the value in the receiving field if necessary). In this book, general formats contain only the options we are using. Comprehensive books and manuals will give a full list of all statements and options.

ADD $\begin{Bmatrix} \text{data-name-1} \\ \text{literal-1} \end{Bmatrix}$ $\begin{Bmatrix} \text{data-name-2} \\ \text{literal-2} \end{Bmatrix}$ ... GIVING data-name-3

SUBTRACT $\begin{Bmatrix} \text{data-name-1} \\ \text{literal-1} \end{Bmatrix}$ ... FROM $\begin{Bmatrix} \text{data-name-2} \\ \text{literal-2} \end{Bmatrix}$ GIVING data-name-3

MULTIPLY $\begin{Bmatrix} \text{data-name-1} \\ \text{literal-1} \end{Bmatrix}$ BY $\begin{Bmatrix} \text{data-name-2} \\ \text{literal-2} \end{Bmatrix}$ GIVING data-name-3

DIVIDE $\begin{Bmatrix} \text{data-name-1} \\ \text{literal-1} \end{Bmatrix}$ INTO $\begin{Bmatrix} \text{data-name-2} \\ \text{literal-2} \end{Bmatrix}$ GIVING data-name-3

DISPLAY $\begin{Bmatrix} \text{data-name} \\ \text{literal} \end{Bmatrix}$ ...

MOVE $\begin{Bmatrix} \text{data-name-1} \\ \text{literal} \end{Bmatrix}$ TO data-name-2

Where there are a series of consecutive data-names and literals in a statement, they may be separated by commas.

Note: In other books and manuals, you may see the term *identifier* instead of data-name in some general formats. The distinction between the two terms is beyond the scope of this book.

Ans 1.11 MOVE and TO are reserved words
33.3 is a literal
NUM-1 and NUM-2 are data-names

Program layout

Rules for laying out a COBOL program are given in Appendix 1. For the moment, we will just look at rules affecting division headings and statements.
Please turn to Appendix 1 (page 109) and note the following:

- columns 8 to 11 form Area A
- columns 12 to 72 form Area B
- division headings must start in Area A (rule 1a)
- statements must be wholly within Area B (rule 2d)

In this book, we will always start division headings (and other Area A entries) at column 8.
We will return to Appendix 1 as further entries are introduced.

◐ **Qu 1.13** Assume a Procedure Division heading starts at column 8 and a statement starts at the beginning of Area B. How many spaces is the statement indented under the division heading?

Running programs   You are reminded that we discussed running programs in the Introduction, and said that a simple program that you might like to run now is given in Appendix 2 (page 110).

Ans 1.12 (a) delete comma and insert BY
 (c) delete BY NUM-3
 (d) replace 3 with a data-name

Summary (Unit 1)

- COBOL programs consist of up to four divisions. Division headings must start in Area A (see Appendix 1) and end with a full stop. The divisions themselves must also end with a full stop.

- The Procedure Division contains statements that are similar in action to statements in BASIC. Statements must be within Area B (see Appendix 1). In this book we will follow a statement with a full stop, although this is sometimes optional.

- Items that are called variables in BASIC are called *fields* in COBOL. Names given to fields are referred to as *data-names*. Rules for formulating data-names are given on page 11.

- Arithmetic statements add, subtract, multiply and divide (general formats on page 14).

- DISPLAY statements display program output on a video screen (general format on page 14).

- MOVE statements assign values to fields (general format on page 14).

- STOP RUN is the last statement executed in Procedure Divisions in this book.

Further questions

1.14 Identify any errors in the following Procedure Division:

```
PROCEDURE DIVISION
    ADD 12 TO 7 GIVING SUM.
    DISPLAY SUM.
    STOP RUN.
```

1.15 The tax rate on the first £200 of pay is zero. All pay above £200 is taxed at 35%. Assuming pay (PAY) does exceed £200, write a Procedure Division that calculates taxable pay (TAXABLE), then calculates tax (TAX), and then displays the tax on the screen. (Multiply by 0.35 to find 35%.)

1.16 A program that calculates electricity charges uses the fields with the following data-names:

```
OLD       for the previous meter reading
NEW       for the present meter reading
UNITS     for the units supplied
CHARGE    for the charge
```

Write a Procedure Division that gives OLD the value 62848 and NEW the value 63178, and then calculates UNITS. The program should then display the values of UNITS and CHARGE on two separate lines of the screen, given that the price per unit is 4 pence.

Answers to Further Questions are given at the end of the book.

Ans 1.13   Four spaces (which is the indentation used in this Unit).

Unit 2 Further statements

This Unit introduces further Procedure Division statements for: inputting data (ACCEPT), decision making (IF), and branching and repetition (PERFORM). Again, many of the principles are similar to those in BASIC (and Pascal and FORTRAN).

ACCEPT statements

The ACCEPT statement allows the user to type in data while a program is running. The action is similar to that of the INPUT statement in BASIC. The following sequence contains an example:

```
ACCEPT NUM.
MULTIPLY NUM BY 2 GIVING PRODUCT.
DISPLAY PRODUCT.
```

When the ACCEPT statement is executed, the program waits until the user types in some data at the keyboard (and then presses the RETURN key).

Suppose the above program is running and the user types in 12. The ACCEPT statement assigns the value of 12 to NUM. Then the MULTIPLY and DISPLAY statements are executed and the number 24 is displayed on the screen.

One general format of the statement in CIS COBOL is:

ACCEPT data-name

So here the ACCEPT statement can include only one data-name (some other COBOL versions allow more than one data-name).

◐ Qu 2.1 Write a sequence that will display the result of adding together three numbers typed in by the user. Use data-names D, E, F and SUM.

IF statements

IF statements are used for making decisions in programs, as in BASIC. Here is an example:

>   IF TAX-CODE = 1 MOVE 0.3 TO TAX-RATE.

which means if TAX-CODE has the value of 1, then assign the value of 0.3 to TAX-RATE. One general format is:

>   IF condition statement . . .

If the condition is satisfied, the statement following the condition is executed. Otherwise the statement is ignored. Some COBOL versions allow the word THEN after the condition (as in BASIC), but we will not use this option here.
Condition forms that can be used in IF statements include:

=	equal to
>	greater than
<	less than
NOT =	not equal to
NOT <	greater than or equal to
NOT >	less than or equal to

Some COBOL versions also allow words such as EQUALS and LESS THAN instead of symbols. Note that the form of the last three conditions is different to that in BASIC.

◐   Qu 2.2   Write a statement that will assign the value of 2.5 to COST if WEIGHT is less than or equal to 30.

COBOL also provides an IF-ELSE option, which many versions of BASIC do not have. The general format is:

>   IF condition statement-1 . . .   ELSE statement-2 . . .

If the condition is true, then statement-1 is executed. Otherwise statement-2 is executed. For example:

>   IF PRICE > 25000 MOVE 0.02 TO DUTY
>   ELSE MOVE 0.01 TO DUTY.

To make programs more readable, the ELSE is often aligned under the IF, as in the above example. Note that however the statement is written, there must be no full stop within the statement but there must be a full stop at the end. In the next example, the statements within the IF statement are indented on separate lines for further clarity:

```
PROCEDURE DIVISION.
    ACCEPT PAY.
    IF PAY > 5000
        MOVE 0.35 TO TAX-RATE       ← no full stop
    ELSE
        MOVE 0.25 TO TAX-RATE.
    DISPLAY TAX-RATE.
    STOP RUN.
```

Qu 2.3 Suppose a program containing the above Procedure Division is running on a computer. What value will be displayed if the user types in (a) 7500 and (b) 5000?

Qu 2.4 When SALES are below £1000, the BONUS is £15. In other cases, BONUS is £45. Write a Procedure Division that will display the value of the bonus on the screen. The user should be able to type in the value of the sales at the time the program is run.

The next example shows several statements following the ELSE. It is taken from a payroll program where all hours worked over 40 are paid at an overtime rate:

```
IF HRS NOT > 40
    MULTIPLY HRS BY RATE GIVING PAY
ELSE
    SUBTRACT 40 FROM HRS GIVING OVERTIME
    MULTIPLY OVERTIME BY OVER-RATE GIVING OVER-PAY
    MULTIPLY 40 BY RATE GIVING BASIC-PAY
    ADD OVER-PAY, BASIC-PAY GIVING PAY.
```

Ans 2.1 ACCEPT D.
       ACCEPT E.
       ACCEPT F.
       ADD D, E, F, GIVING SUM.
       DISPLAY SUM.

It is possible for a statement following the condition to itself be an IF statement. This second IF statement is then said to be *nested*. The next example includes a nested IF statement:

```
IF CODE = 1
    DISPLAY RATE1
ELSE
    IF CODE = 2
        DISPLAY RATE2
    ELSE
        DISPLAY RATE0.
```

← nested IF statement

Here, if CODE equals 1 or 2, the program displays the value of RATE1 or RATE2 respectively. If CODE has any other value, the program prints out the value of RATE0. Again, note there is no full stop within the IF statement.

Further nesting can occur and great care must be taken on layout. In this book, we will adopt the layout given above for nested IF statements. Other layouts may be used — some better than others — and you may like to try experimenting when you become more proficient.

The next program provides a simple guessing game, in which the 'player' is asked to type a number (say between 1 and 50). The player 'wins' if he types a lucky number. In this program the lucky numbers are 17, 45, and 47. Note that the statement DISPLAY 0 will display a zero on the screen.

```
ACCEPT N.
IF N = 17
    DISPLAY N
ELSE
    IF N = 45
        DISPLAY N
    ELSE
        IF N = 47
            DISPLAY N
        ELSE
            DISPLAY 0.
```

Ans 2.2 IF WEIGHT NOT > 30 MOVE 2.5 TO COST.

◐ **Qu 2.5** Suppose a program containing the above sequence is running on a computer. What number will be displayed if a player types in (a) 44, (b) 45 or (c) 46?

◐ **Qu 2.6** Write a sequence for a similar guessing game with the following lucky numbers: 13, any number below 10, and any number above 45. If the player hits a lucky number, that number should be displayed. Otherwise zero should be displayed.

Some versions of COBOL allow compound conditions in IF statements, by including the words AND and OR in the condition. For example, the IF statement in the last sequence above could be written as:

```
IF N = 17 OR N = 45 OR N = 47
    DISPLAY N
ELSE
    DISPLAY 0.
```

However, not all COBOL versions provide compound conditions and we will not consider them further in this book.

Ans 2.3 (a) 0.35   (b) 0.25

Ans 2.4 PROCEDURE DIVISION.
```
        ACCEPT SALES.
        IF SALES < 1000
            MOVE 15 TO BONUS
        ELSE
            MOVE 45 TO BONUS.
        DISPLAY BONUS.
        STOP RUN.
```

Paragraphs

Before going on to further statements, we need to introduce the concept of a *paragraph*. A paragraph consists of one or more statements headed by a name. Turn to the program on page 77. The Procedure Division here contains four paragraphs, for example the first paragraph is called ANALYSIS and the second is called YES-REPLIES.

Paragraph-names must start in Area A (see Appendix 1, rule 1c) and must end with a full stop. The last statement in a paragraph must also end with a full stop.

Rules for making up paragraph-names are the same as those for data-names (see page 11), except that paragraph-names can consist entirely of digits.

◐ Qu 2.7   What is the name of the last paragraph in the Procedure Division on page 77?

Note: Unlike CIS COBOL, some versions of COBOL require that all statements be in paragraphs, hence a Procedure Division cannot start with a statement.

PERFORM statements and branching

The PERFORM statement is used to branch to another part of the program. One general format is:

    PERFORM paragraph-name

The program branches to the specified paragraph, executes all the statements in the paragraph, and then returns to the statement that follows the PERFORM statement.
    For example, consider the following sequence:

```
ACCEPT ORDER.
PERFORM PROCESS.
DISPLAY COST.
```

When the value of ORDER has been input, the program will branch to a paragraph called PROCESS, execute the statements in the PROCESS paragraph, and then execute the DISPLAY COST statement.
    This branching action of the PERFORM statement is similar to that of a GOTO statement in BASIC, except that the PERFORM statement automatically returns to the statement following the branch. (In fact, the equivalent statement in BASIC is GOSUB.)

◐ **Qu 2.8** Turn to the program on page 77. What is the next statement executed (a) after PERFORM DISPLAY-RESULTS, and (b) after the last statement on the page?

◐ **Qu 2.9** Write a statement that will branch to a paragraph called RE-ORDER if stock is less than 500. After the last statement in the RE-ORDER paragraph, the program should execute the statement following the branch. Use a field called STOCK.

Ans 2.5 (a) 0 (b) 45 (c) 0

Ans 2.6 ACCEPT N.
```
    IF N = 13
        DISPLAY N
    ELSE
        IF N < 10
            DISPLAY N
        ELSE
            IF N > 45
                DISPLAY N
            ELSE
                DISPLAY 0.
```

Arithmetic statement formats

This is a convenient point to introduce alternative formats for arithmetic statements. All arithmetic statements up to now have included the word GIVING, and so are often called the *giving* option. Alternative formats are shown below:

ADD $\begin{Bmatrix} \text{data-name-1} \\ \text{literal} \end{Bmatrix}$ ... TO data-name-2

SUBTRACT $\begin{Bmatrix} \text{data-name-1} \\ \text{literal} \end{Bmatrix}$ ... FROM data-name-2

MULTIPLY $\begin{Bmatrix} \text{data-name-1} \\ \text{literal} \end{Bmatrix}$ BY data-name-2

DIVIDE $\begin{Bmatrix} \text{data-name-1} \\ \text{literal} \end{Bmatrix}$ INTO data-name-2

Here are some examples:

```
ADD X TO Y.
SUBTRACT X FROM Y.
MULTIPLY X BY Y.
DIVIDE X INTO Y.
```

In all these examples, the answer is placed in Y. That is, Y is the receiving field. In the ADD statement, X is added to Y and the result is placed in Y; hence the original value of Y is lost. For example, if $X = 3$ and $Y = 15$ before execution of the ADD statement, then after execution $X = 3$ and $Y = 18$.

◐ Qu 2.10   If $X = 3$ and $Y = 15$, give the value of X and Y after execution of the above (a) SUBTRACT, (b) MULTIPLY and (c) DIVIDE statements.

Ans 2.7   DISPLAY-RESULTS

The ADD statement is particularly useful. For example:

>   ADD PAY TO TOTAL-PAY.
>   ADD MARKS1, MARKS2, MARKS3 TO TOTAL-MARKS.
>   ADD 1 TO C.

The last statement would be written in BASIC as:

>   LET C = C + 1

◐ Qu 2.11 Write statements that will (a) increment COUNTER by one, (b) increase SCORE by 15, (c) add NUM1 to NUM2 and place the result in NUM1, (d) find the result of A/B and place it in A, (e) double the value of BET.

PERFORM statements and repetition

Consider the following Procedure Division:

>   PROCEDURE DIVISION.
>   MOVE 1 TO NUM.
>   DISPLAY NUM.
>   ADD 2 TO NUM.
>   DISPLAY NUM.
>   ADD 2 TO NUM.
>   DISPLAY NUM.
>   ADD 2 TO NUM.
>   DISPLAY NUM.
>   STOP RUN.

◐ Qu 2.12 What numbers will be displayed when a program with the above Procedure Division is run?

Ans 2.8 (a) DISPLAY SPACE UPON CRT.
        (b) CLOSE DATA-FILE.

Ans 2.9 IF STOCK < 500 PERFORM RE-ORDER.

We can avoid repeating statements by setting up a loop using the PERFORM-UNTIL statement. An alternative way of writing the Procedure Division above then becomes:

```
PROCEDURE DIVISION.
    MOVE 1 TO NUM.
    PERFORM SERIES UNTIL NUM > 7.
    STOP RUN.
SERIES.
    DISPLAY NUM.
    ADD 2 TO NUM.
```

The SERIES paragraph is executed repeatedly until the value of NUM exceeds 7. Then the statement following the PERFORM statement is executed (which here is STOP RUN).

The general format of the PERFORM-UNTIL statement is:

PERFORM paragraph-name UNTIL condition

where the condition forms are as listed on page 19. The specified paragraph is executed repeatedly until the condition is satisfied.

Note carefully in the Procedure Division above that although NUM has the value 9 at the end of the last loop, the number 9 is not displayed. The next example contains a similar loop:

```
PROCEDURE DIVISION.
    MOVE 5 TO NUM.
    PERFORM LOOP UNTIL NUM > 100.
    STOP RUN.
LOOP.
    DISPLAY NUM.
    ADD 5 TO NUM.
```

◐ Qu 2.13 What values will be displayed when a program with the above Procedure Division is run?

◐ Qu 2.14 Write a Procedure Division that will display every even value between 2 and 1000 inclusive. Use a field called NUM and a paragraph called SERIES.

Ans 2.10 (a) X = 3   Y = 12
          (b) X = 3   Y = 45
          (c) X = 3   Y = 5

Summary (Unit 2)

- The ACCEPT statement allows input to a program from the keyboard. A general format is:

    <u>ACCEPT</u> data-name

- The IF statement is used for making decisions. The general format is:

    <u>IF</u> condition statement-1 . . .   [<u>ELSE</u> statement-2 . . .]

    If the condition is satisfied, then statement-1 is executed. Otherwise statement-2 is executed (if present). The complete IF statement must end with a full stop, but there must be no full stop within the statement. Condition forms are given on page 19.

- A paragraph consists of one or more statements headed by a name. This paragraph name must start in Area A (see Appendix 1) and end with a full stop. The paragraph itself must also end with a full stop.

- The PERFORM statement is used for branching and repetition. One general format is:

    <u>PERFORM</u> paragraph-name   [<u>UNTIL</u> condition]

    The program executes the specified paragraph, and then returns to the statement following the PERFORM statement. If the UNTIL option is present, the specified paragraph is executed repeatedly until the condition is satisfied.

- Alternative arithmetic statement formats are given on page 25. The ADD statement is particularly useful.

Ans 2.11   (a) ADD 1 TO COUNTER.
           (b) ADD 15 TO SCORE.
           (c) ADD NUM2 TO NUM1.
           (d) DIVIDE B INTO A.
           (e) MULTIPLY 2 BY BET.

Ans 2.12   1, 3, 5 and 7

Further questions

2.15 Write a paragraph called HIGHER that will display the higher of two unequal numbers typed in by the user. Use data-names C and D.

2.16 Write a Procedure Division for a program that allows the user to type in marks gained by a candidate in three tests (use data-names MARKS1, MARKS2 and MARKS3). The program should add the marks together to obtain the total marks (TOT-MARKS). The passmark is 45. The program should display the total only if it equals or exceeds the passmark.

2.17 When a program with the Procedure Division below is run, what numbers will be displayed?

```
PROCEDURE DIVISION.
    MOVE 100 TO NUM.
    PERFORM LOOP UNTIL NUM > 250.
    STOP RUN.
LOOP.
    DISPLAY NUM.
    ADD 1 TO NUM.
```

Ans 2.13 Every fifth number between 5 and 100 inclusive

Ans 2.14
```
PROCEDURE DIVISION.
    MOVE 2 TO NUM.
    PERFORM SERIES UNTIL NUM > 1000.
    STOP RUN.
SERIES.
    DISPLAY NUM.
    ADD 2 TO NUM.
```

Unit 3 Text and screen displays

Up to now the programs we have looked at have dealt with *numbers* only. For example: DISPLAY statements have printed numbers; MOVE statements have assigned numbers to fields; and IF statements have compared one number to another.

Now we consider *text*. When the following statement is executed:

    DISPLAY "TAX RATE".

the text TAX RATE will appear on the screen. As in BASIC, all text or characters enclosed by quotes are printed out as they stand — including spaces. (Here we are using double quotes, but some COBOL versions require single quotes.)

The text TAX RATE is called a *literal* in COBOL because it is interpreted literally by the computer. In earlier programs, we saw numbers as examples of literals (page 11). To distinguish between the two types, numbers are called numeric literals and text called alphanumeric literals. In BASIC, alphanumeric literals are called character strings.

Unlike numeric literals, alphanumeric literals must be enclosed in quotes. The following sequence contains examples:

    DISPLAY "TYPE DOLLARS".
    ACCEPT DOLLARS.
    MULTIPLY DOLLARS BY 5 GIVING FRANCS.
    DISPLAY "NUMBER OF FRANCS = ", FRANCS.

◐   Qu 3.1   In the above sequence identify (a) numeric literals, (b) alphanumeric literals.

◐   Qu 3.2   Write a statement that will display the text TYPE EXCHANGE RATE on the screen.

Note: Alphanumeric literals are often called non-numeric literals.

Alphanumeric fields Up to now all fields have held numbers. These are called numeric fields (and are equivalent to numeric variables in BASIC). Fields can also hold text. These are called alphanumeric fields (and are equivalent to string variables in BASIC).

In BASIC, numeric and string variables are distinguished by adding a $ sign to string variable names. In COBOL, numeric and alphanumeric fields are distinguished by entries in another division, as we will see in the next Unit.

Assuming NAME, ADDRESS and DATE have been defined as alphanumeric fields, we can write statements like:

```
MOVE "M. J. OATEY" TO NAME.
MOVE "103 BOROUGH RD., LONDON SE1" TO ADDRESS.
IF DATE = "17/11/60" DISPLAY "BIRTHDAY WINNER".
```

again enclosing the alphanumeric literals in double quotes.

◐ Qu 3.3   Write a statement that will display CORRECT on the screen if an alphanumeric field called ANSWER holds the value PARIS.

As in BASIC, arithmetic can be carried out only on numeric fields and literals. You must be particularly careful to distinguish between alphanumeric literals containing digits and numeric literals. An alphanumeric literal can contain any characters. A numeric literal can contain only digits, a decimal point, and a plus or minus sign; if any other characters are present the literal becomes alphanumeric. Here are some examples:

Numeric	*Alphanumeric*
20000	20,000
+23	+ 23
67.5	£67.5
	FUV 727A

We have seen the general format of the MOVE statement is:

MOVE $\begin{Bmatrix} \text{data-name-1} \\ \text{literal} \end{Bmatrix}$ TO data-name-2 . . .

Here the sending and receiving items should be of the same type. For example, if the data-name-1 field is numeric, the data-name-2 field should also be numeric; or if the literal is alphanumeric, the data-name-2 field should be alphanumeric. There are some rules for mixed type moves, but the novice is advised to avoid them and we will not use them in this book.

◐ Qu 3.4   In the following statements NUM is a numeric field and ALPHANUM is an alphanumeric field. Assuming mixed type moves are not allowed, identify any errors.
(a) MOVE 100,000 TO NUM.
(b) MOVE 30 TO ALPHANUM.
(c) MOVE −2.45 TO NUM.
(d) MOVE "123A" TO ALPHANUM.
(e) SUBTRACT 10 FROM NUM.
(f) SUBTRACT 10 FROM ALPHANUM GIVING NUM.

In COBOL it is possible to use a third type of field besides numeric and alphanumeric. This is an *alphabetic* field, which can hold only letters and spaces (unlike alphanumeric fields, which can hold any characters). Alphabetic fields are not commonly used. For example, the NAME, ADDRESS and DATE fields above all contain non-alphabetic characters like commas and slashes. Even surnames can contain commas or hyphens (e.g. SUTTON-SMITH). We will not use alphabetic fields in this book.

Ans 3.1   (a) 5
(b) "TYPE DOLLARS" and "NUMBER OF FRANCS = "

Ans 3.2   DISPLAY "TYPE EXCHANGE RATE".

Figurative literals Two special literal forms are ZERO and SPACE. These are called figurative literals or figurative constants. Here are two examples of their use:

    MOVE ZERO TO NUM.
    MOVE SPACE TO ALPHANUM.

The first statement will fill the NUM field with zeros. The second statement will fill ALPHANUM with spaces. ZERO should be used with numeric fields, and SPACE with alphanumeric fields.

Before accepting an entry from the screen, it is sometimes necessary to clear out the current value from a field (for reasons given later). For example, to accept an entry from the screen into an alphanumeric field called NAME, we may write:

    MOVE SPACE TO NAME.
    ACCEPT NAME.

Another use of SPACE is to clear the screen. The statement:

    DISPLAY SPACE UPON CRT.

can always be used to clear the screen in CIS COBOL (where CRT refers to a microcomputer or terminal screen). Other COBOL versions may have different methods of clearing the screen.

◐   **Qu 3.5** A program accepts an entry from the screen into an alphanumeric field called TOWN. Write a sequence of statements that will clear the screen, then clear out the current value in TOWN, and then accept the new entry.

Note: At the start of a program, some COBOL versions (including CIS COBOL) automatically set numeric fields to zero and alphanumeric fields to spaces. Other versions do not. In any event, it is considered bad practice to assume such automatic initialization, and we will not assume initial values in this book.

Ans 3.3 IF ANSWER = "PARIS" DISPLAY "CORRECT".

Repetitive processing

We can now consider an approach to repeatedly processing data. The Procedure Division below converts dollars to francs given a hypothetical exchange rate of five francs to the dollar. The line starting with an asterisk is a comment (equivalent to a REM statement in BASIC, see Appendix 1 rule 4a noting the column 7 position).

```
PROCEDURE DIVISION.
    MOVE SPACE TO ANS.
    PERFORM CONVERSION UNTIL ANS = "N".
    STOP RUN.
CONVERSION.
    DISPLAY "Type number of dollars".
    ACCEPT DOLLARS.
    MULTIPLY DOLLARS BY 5 GIVING FRANCS.
    DISPLAY "Number of francs = ", FRANCS.
*more data?
    DISPLAY "Another conversion? Y/N".
    ACCEPT ANS.
```

loop ends when answer is N

The CONVERSION paragraph is executed repeatedly while the user replies Y to the prompt about another conversion. When the reply is N, the program breaks out of the loop and stops.

Note that ANS is given an initial value of a space. This is because we are not assuming automatic initialization, and we need to ensure ANS has a value other than N at the start of the program.

The alphanumeric literals in the DISPLAY statements are in lower case, which can make a program and its output more readable. However, some systems may not provide lower case characters, so the whole program must be in upper case. (Note that in the main text of this book, we will still print prompts in upper case for clarity.)

◐ **Qu 3.6** State whether each field in the above Procedure Division is numeric or alphanumeric.

◐ **Qu 3.7** Write a Procedure Division that can repeatedly convert kilograms to pounds weight, given that one kilogram equals 2.2 pounds. Use the same approach as that shown above, with fields called KILOS, POUNDS and ANS, and a paragraph called LOOP.

Ans 3.4 (a) comma is illegal (in a numeric value)
(b) 30 should be enclosed by quotes
(c) ALPHANUM cannot be used in arithmetic

Totals

Repetitive processing often involves calculating running totals. For example, the currency conversion program may keep running totals of money taken in and paid out (which could be used to check cash balances at the end of the day).

A general approach to keeping totals is shown by the following Procedure Division, which keeps a running total of dollars taken in:

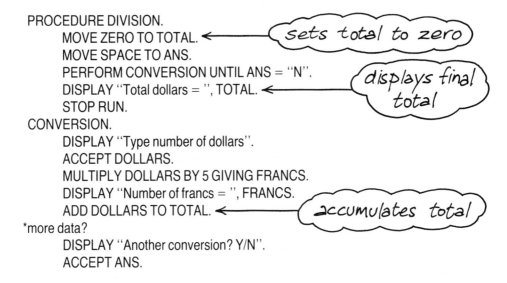

```
PROCEDURE DIVISION.
    MOVE ZERO TO TOTAL.          ← sets total to zero
    MOVE SPACE TO ANS.
    PERFORM CONVERSION UNTIL ANS = "N".
    DISPLAY "Total dollars = ", TOTAL.   ← displays final total
    STOP RUN.
CONVERSION.
    DISPLAY "Type number of dollars".
    ACCEPT DOLLARS.
    MULTIPLY DOLLARS BY 5 GIVING FRANCS.
    DISPLAY "Number of francs = ", FRANCS.
    ADD DOLLARS TO TOTAL.        ← accumulates total
*more data?
    DISPLAY "Another conversion? Y/N".
    ACCEPT ANS.
```

Notice that TOTAL is set to zero initially. Again we are not assuming automatic initialization in this book, and we must ensure that TOTAL starts with a value of zero.

◐ Qu 3.8 Write a Procedure Division that keeps a running total of numbers typed in by the user. The current value of the total should be displayed after each number is input. Use fields called NUM, TOT-NUM and ANS, and a paragraph called DATA-IN.

Ans 3.5 DISPLAY SPACE UPON CRT.
         MOVE SPACE TO TOWN.
         ACCEPT TOWN.

Cursor position

When ACCEPT and DISPLAY statements are executed, we have assumed the cursor is positioned at the start of the next line on the screen. This may not be the case, depending on the COBOL version, on how the system has been set up (configured), and on entries in another COBOL division (the Environment Division). For example, in CIS COBOL the cursor may move to the home position (top left of the screen) after an ACCEPT statement is executed.

Further, most microcomputer versions of COBOL allow you to specify the cursor position in ACCEPT and DISPLAY statements. In CIS COBOL, the format for the ACCEPT statement is:

    ACCEPT data-name AT nnnn

where nnnn is a four digit number specifying the cursor position. The first two digits specify the line and the second two specify the position on the line (both starting at 01). So 0101 specifies the home position, and 0201 the start of the second line. The following statement:

    ACCEPT NUM AT 0415.

will accept an entry on the fourth line at character position 15.

The format for the DISPLAY statement is:

    DISPLAY   {data-name}   AT nnnn
              {literal   }

With the AT option, you can include only one data-name or literal (compare this to the DISPLAY format on page 14).

Ans 3.6   ANS is alphanumeric. DOLLARS and FRANCS are numeric (because they are used in arithmetic).

Ans 3.7   PROCEDURE DIVISION.
              MOVE SPACE TO ANS.
              PERFORM LOOP UNTIL ANS = "N".
              STOP RUN.
          LOOP.
              DISPLAY "Type number of kilograms".
              ACCEPT KILOS.
              MULTIPLY KILOS BY 2.2 GIVING POUNDS.
              DISPLAY "Number of pounds = ", POUNDS.
          *more data?
              DISPLAY "Another conversion? Y/N".
              ACCEPT ANS.

As stated above, ACCEPT and DISPLAY statements can have varying effects. This is particularly true of ACCEPT statements without the AT option in CIS COBOL. From now on in programs that accept input from the screen, we will normally use the AT option. When you answer questions, clear the screen, start all entries at position 10, and use every other line (unless otherwise stated). Where text precedes a field, separate the text and field by two spaces. For example, part of the Procedure Division on page 34 would now be:

```
DISPLAY SPACE UPON CRT.      ← remember to clear the screen
DISPLAY "Type number of dollars" AT 0110.
ACCEPT DOLLARS AT 0134.
MULTIPLY DOLLARS BY 5 GIVING FRANCS.
DISPLAY "Number of francs" AT 0310.
DISPLAY FRANCS AT 0328.
```

◐ Qu 3.9 Rewrite other statements in the Procedure Division on page 34 using the AT option as appropriate.

Ans 3.8
```
       PROCEDURE DIVISION.
           MOVE ZERO TO TOT-NUM.
           MOVE SPACE TO ANS.
           PERFORM DATA-IN UNTIL ANS = "N".
           STOP RUN.
       DATA-IN.
           DISPLAY "Type a number".
           ACCEPT NUM.
           ADD NUM TO TOT-NUM.
           DISPLAY "Total = ", TOT-NUM.
      *more data?
           DISPLAY "Another number? Y/N".
           ACCEPT ANS.
```

Summary (Unit 3)

- A *literal* is an element in a statement that is interpreted literally by the computer. There are two main types: numbers or numeric literals, and text or alphanumeric literals. Alphanumeric literals are sometimes called non-numeric literals.

- Rules for using literals are:

Numeric	*Alphanumeric*
can include only digits, a decimal point, and a plus or minus sign	can include any characters
must not be enclosed in quotes	must be enclosed in quotes
should be assigned to numeric fields	should be assigned to alphanumeric fields
can be used in arithmetic	cannot be used in arithmetic

- Numeric and alphanumeric fields are distinguished by entries in the Data Division (see Unit 4).

- Two special *figurative* literals are ZERO and SPACE. These are used to fill a field with zeros or spaces respectively. The statement DISPLAY SPACE UPON CRT clears the screen in CIS COBOL.

- Repetitive processing loops can be set up using the PERFORM-UNTIL statement.

- In most microcomputer versions of COBOL, the cursor position can be specified in the ACCEPT and DISPLAY statements. In CIS COBOL the AT format is used (see page 36).

Further questions

3.10 Modify the Procedure Division on page 34 so that the user can type in the current exchange rate. The rate need be typed once only, using a field called EX-RATE. Do not use the AT option.

3.11 Rewrite the Procedure Division on page 35 so that when all the numbers have been typed, the average will be displayed. Use additional fields called COUNTER and AVERAGE. Clear the screen and use the AT option (as described on page 37).

Note: Exercise A, which follows, gives further practice in using repetitive processing loops.

Ans 3.9 DISPLAY "Another conversion? Y/N" at 0510.
 ACCEPT ANS AT 0535.

Exercise A

These exercises are designed to consolidate the material in Units 1 to 3.

Exercise A-1

The following Procedure Division will calculate hotel costs, given the number of NIGHTS and the RATE per night. For two nights or less the rate is £12 per night. For up to six nights the rate is £10. For more than six nights the rate is £8 per night.

```
PROCEDURE DIVISION.
    MOVE SPACE TO ANS.
    PERFORM COSTS UNTIL ANS = "N".
    STOP RUN.
COSTS.
    DISPLAY SPACE UPON CRT.
    DISPLAY "Type number of nights" AT 0110.
    ACCEPT NIGHTS AT 0133.
    IF  NIGHTS NOT > 2
        MOVE 12 TO RATE
    ELSE
        IF  NIGHTS NOT > 6
            MOVE 10 TO RATE
        ELSE
            MOVE 8 TO RATE.
    MULTIPLY NIGHTS BY RATE GIVING CHARGE.
    DISPLAY "Charge" AT 0310.
    DISPLAY CHARGE AT 0318.
*more data?
    DISPLAY "Another bill? Y/N" AT 1210.
    ACCEPT ANS AT 1229.
```

Suppose a program with this Procedure Division is running. What will be displayed if the user types (a) 11 and (b) 6?

Answers to Exercises are at the end of the book.

Exercise A-2

A hotel has the following charges:

1 night	£15
up to 7 nights	£12
up to 28 nights	£10
over 28 nights	£7

Write a Procedure Division that will calculate charges, using the same fields and approach as in Exercise A-1. However, when the user replies N to the ANOTHER BILL? prompt, the program should display the total of all nights stayed (TOT-NIGHTS) and the total of all charges (TOT-CHARGE) on lines 5 and 7 of the screen.

Exercise A-3

An employee receives £2 for all hours worked up to 40. The *next* 10 hours, if any, are paid at £3, and the remainder at £4 per hour. Write a Procedure Divison that will display the total pay for the one employee (do not use a loop). Use fields called HRS, PAY and HIGH-PAY.

Unit 4 Field descriptions

We turn now to another division in COBOL, the Data Division. Among other things, the Data Division contains definitions of all fields used in the Procedure Division.

Fields are defined by *field descriptions*. Three descriptions are given below for fields with data-names NUM-1, NUM-2 and DAY:

```
01   NUM-1     PICTURE 99.
01   NUM-2     PICTURE 99999.
01   DAY       PICTURE XXX.
```

All these entries start with the number 01, which is called the *level number*. We will return to its purpose in the next Unit; for the moment all field descriptions will start with the number 01. The level number is followed by the field data-name.

The last element in the above field descriptions is a *picture* clause (followed by a full stop). These picture clauses define the type and size of the fields. The symbol 9 shows a numeric field, and the symbol X shows an alphanumeric (string) field. The number of 9 and X symbols shows the size of the field. So:

```
NUM-1   is a numeric field, two characters long
NUM-2   is a numeric field, five characters long
DAY     is an alphanumeric field, three characters long
```

The word PICTURE is usually shortened to PIC, as in the following field descriptions:

```
01   TAX-CODE   PIC XXXX.
01   AMOUNT     PIC 999999.
```

◐ Qu 4.1   State the type and size of the fields (a) TAX-CODE and (b) AMOUNT.

To avoid numerous symbols in picture clauses, the field size can be placed in brackets after a single symbol, for example:

    PIC X(10)   instead of PIC XXXXXXXXXX
    PIC 9(6)   instead of PIC 999999
    PIC 9(2)   instead of PIC 99

though obviously in the last example it is shorter simply to use PIC 99.

◐ Qu 4.2 Write picture clauses for the following fields using the shortest form: (a) numeric, 7 characters; (b) alphanumeric, 1 character; (c) numeric, 3 characters; (d) alphanumeric, 65 characters.

Numeric fields defined so far can hold only integer (whole) numbers, not decimal numbers. Decimal numbers are more complicated and we will look at them in Unit 8. So for the present we can use only integer numbers (hence money values must be expressed in pence, e.g. 842 pence rather than £8.42).

Field sizes must be big enough for the maximum number of characters the fields may have to hold. Suppose a program contains the statement:

    ADD 500, ITEM GIVING RESULT.

and ITEM can hold a four-figure number. The maximum that ITEM may have to hold is 9999, so the maximum that RESULT may have to hold is 10499. So RESULT must be a PIC 9(5) field. (Refer to more comprehensive COBOL books or manuals for the effects of size errors.)

Now consider this statement:

    MULTIPLY NUM BY 100 GIVING PRODUCT.

◐ Qu 4.3 Assuming NUM is a PIC 999 field, write a picture clause for PRODUCT.

The Data Division and complete programs

We now give a complete Data Division for a program that uses two fields called NAME and AGE:

```
DATA DIVISION.
WORKING-STORAGE SECTION.
01    NAME         PIC X(20).
01    AGE          PIC 99.
```

The first line contains the division heading, which must end with a full stop (like the Procedure Division heading).

The second line contains a section heading. Every Data Division consists of one or more sections, and the above division consists of a Working-Storage Section. The significance of the name will become clear later when we look at another section in the Data Division. For the present, all Data Divisions will consist of a Working-Storage Section.

Notice the hyphen in WORKING-STORAGE. All section headings must start in Area A (see Appendix 1, rule 1b) and must end with a full stop.

The third and fourth lines above contain field descriptions. The level number must start in Area A (see Appendix 1, rule 1e) and the rest of field description must be in Area B (rule 2c). There must be at least one space between the data-name and the picture clause, but picture clauses are normally aligned for ease of reading. Each field description must end with a full stop.

◐ Qu 4.4 Write a complete Data Division for a program that uses two fields: MODEL (alphanumeric, 10 characters) and PRICE (numeric, 6 characters).

Ans 4.1   (a) alphanumeric, 4 characters
          (b) numeric, 6 characters

We now add a Data Division to the Procedure Division we gave at the beginning of Unit 1 (page 4):

```
DATA DIVISION.
WORKING-STORAGE SECTION.
01    A              PIC 99.

PROCEDURE DIVISION.
    MULTIPLY 22 BY 4 GIVING A.
    DISPLAY A.
    STOP RUN.
```

The Data Division always comes before the Procedure Division in programs. We have left a line space between the two divisions, but this is not mandatory.

We have now seen examples of the Data Division and the Procedure Division. The other two COBOL divisions are:

Identification Division   which includes information like the program name and author name

Environment Division   which includes information on the hardware used to run the program

Some COBOL versions require all four divisions in every program. However, in CIS COBOL the Identification Division can always be omitted, and the Environment and Data Divisions can be omitted if no entries are required. In practice, nearly all programs require a Data Division (to define fields), and programs often require an Environment Division, as we will see later. However, the above Data and Procedure Divisions do not require an Environment Division and so form a complete program in CIS COBOL.

For COBOL versions that require all four divisions, entries for the Identification and Environment Divisions are given in Appendix 2, page 110.

Ans 4.2   (a) PIC 9(7)   (b) PIC X   (c) PIC 9(3) or PIC 999   (d) PIC X(65)

Ans 4.3   PIC 9(5)

Running programs The rest of Appendix 2 gives details of running programs. When you have access to a computer, the first program you could run is the very simple program at the beginning of the Appendix (page 110), as suggested earlier. You might then run the program on the previous page above.

You can also add a Data Division to other Procedure Divisions or sequences given earlier in the book. Remember that you can use only integer values for the present, so you may need to change some numbers in programs in order to run them (e.g. the Procedure Division on page 20).

With programs using the ACCEPT statement in CIS COBOL, you should clear the screen and use the AT option. For example, the sequence on page 18 could be included in a program as follows:

```
DATA DIVISION.
WORKING-STORAGE SECTION.
01   NUM         PIC 9(3).
01   PRODUCT     PIC 9(4).

PROCEDURE DIVISION.
     DISPLAY SPACE UPON CRT.
     ACCEPT NUM AT 0110.
     MULTIPLY NUM BY 2 GIVING PRODUCT.
     DISPLAY NUM AT 0310.
     STOP RUN.
```

Also, before running programs using an ACCEPT statement, you should read the following section on screen input.

Notice that in the above program we have made PRODUCT a PIC 9(4) field for the maximum number it may have to hold.

◐ Qu 4.5 Write a Data Division that defines the fields in the Procedure Division on page 34, assuming the largest number of dollars input is under 100,000.

Ans 4.4   DATA DIVISION.
          WORKING-STORAGE SECTION.
          01   MODEL   PIC X(10).
          01   PRICE   PIC 9(6).

Screen input

When entering numbers from the screen into a numeric field in CIS COBOL, you must type leading zeros. The reason is that characters are entered from the left side of a field. For example, take a PIC 999 field with an initial value of zero:

| 0 | 0 | 0 |

If you type 46, the characters are entered as follows:

| 4 | 6 | 0 |

giving a value of 460. If you want the value 46, you must type 046:

| 0 | 4 | 6 |

Here are some more examples for a PIC 999 field:

characters typed	value stored
123	123
12	120
1	100
01	10
001	1

◐ **Qu 4.6** If the following entries are typed from the screen into a PIC 9(5) field, what values are stored: (a) 12345, (b) 123, (c) 00600, (d) 2, (e) 00002

Note: The need to type leading zeros can obviously lead to errors, particular with inexperienced users. A method of preventing these errors is briefly mentioned on page 106.

The following program is useful in demonstrating screen input and output:

```
DATA DIVISION.
WORKING-STORAGE SECTION.
01   NUM        PIC9 (4).
01   ANS        PIC X.

PROCEDURE DIVISION.
     MOVE SPACE TO ANS.
     PERFORM DEMO UNTIL ANS = "N".
     STOP RUN.
DEMO.
     DISPLAY SPACE UPON CRT.
     MOVE ZERO TO NUM.
     ACCEPT NUM AT 0110.
     ADD 8 TO NUM.
     DISPLAY NUM AT 0310.
     DISPLAY "Another number?" AT 0510.
     ACCEPT ANS AT 0527.
```

In an operation on a field, a program will use the stored value and will include leading and trailing spaces when displaying results. For example, if the above program is running and you type 50 (on the first line of the screen), the program will display 5008 (on the third line). And if you type 0005, the program will display 0013.

◐ Qu 4.7 If you type the following, what will the program display? (a) 1234, (b) 123, (c) 12, (d) 1, (e) 02, (f) 0002.

Ans 4.5 DATA DIVISION.
         WORKING-STORAGE SECTION.
         01   DOLLARS   PIC 9(5).
         01   FRANCS   PIC 9(6).
         01   ANS   PIC X.

We now explain the reason for the statement in the above program:

> MOVE ZERO TO NUM.

In CIS COBOL, characters are entered individually from the screen (starting from the left of a field, as we have already seen). When making a new entry, any characters already in a field that are not overwritten may remain. For example, suppose a PIC X(6) field holds the following:

| B | I | R | O | S | |

and a new entry INK is accepted from the screen without clearing the old value. The field would now hold:

| I | N | K | O | S | |

Only the first three characters are overwritten.

So if there is a possibility that input from the screen may not overwrite the current contents of a field, you must clear that field in CIS COBOL. Some other COBOL versions do not have this requirement (try running the above program without the MOVE ZERO TO NUM statement).

Numeric fields are cleared by moving ZERO to the field. Alphanumeric fields are cleared by moving SPACE to the field.

◐ **Qu 4.8** Suppose a field holds INKOS as shown above. If the program does not clear the field and the user now inputs ** (two asterisks), what value is held in the field?

Note: The need for leading zeros or clearing fields applies only when entering values from the screen. It does not apply when assigning values using MOVE statements (or to input from disk files, which we will use later).

Ans 4.6 (a) 12345 (b) 12300 (c) 600 (d) 20000 (e) 2

Summary (Unit 4)

- Fields must be defined in the Data Division. A field description takes the form:

    level-number   data-name   PIC   picture

- Individual fields take the level number 01, which must start in Area A. The rest of the entry must be in Area B and must end with a full stop.

- In the picture, 9 symbols show a numeric field and X symbols show an alphanumeric field. The number of symbols shows the size of the field.

- The Data Division contains one or more sections. All section headings start in Area A and end with a full stop. Individual fields can be defined in the Working-Storage Section (note the hyphen).

- The remaining two COBOL divisions are the Identification and Environment Divisions. Unlike CIS COBOL, some versions require all four divisions in each program (see Appendix 2).

- When entering numeric input from the screen, you must type leading zeros in CIS COBOL. Some other versions do not have this requirement.

- If input from the screen may not overwrite the current contents of a field, you must clear the field in CIS COBOL. Some other versions do not have this requirement.

Ans 4.7   (a) 1242   (b) 1238   (c) 1208   (d) 1008   (e) 0208   (f) 0010

Further questions

4.9 Write a Data Division that defines the fields used in the Procedure Division in Qu 1.16. Assume meter readings do not exceed 99999.

4.10 Write a complete program in CIS COBOL that includes the paragraph in Qu 2.15 (using the AT option). Assume numbers are under 100.

4.11 Write a Data Division that defines the fields in the Procedure Division in Exercise A-2 (page 39) with the addition of a field called NAME for the customer name (maximum 20 characters). Assume the nights stayed do not exceed 99 and the number of customers do not exceed 999.

Ans 4.8   **KOS

Unit 5 Record descriptions

A record consists of one or more fields. Using records allows groups of related fields to be dealt with as a whole, rather than dealing with each individual field separately.

A payroll record could contain fields as follows:

PAY-RECORD		
NAME	HOURS	RATE

The name of the record is PAY-RECORD and it consists of three fields: NAME, HOURS and RATE. Sometimes further sub-divisions are made, as in the QTY field in the following record called STOCK-RECORD:

STOCK-RECORD			
PART-NO	QTY		PRICE
	OLD-STOCK	NEW-STOCK	

In COBOL, the structure of PAY-RECORD would be described by the following entries in the DATA Division (omitting picture clauses for the moment):

```
01  PAY-RECORD
    02  NAME
    02  HOURS
    02  RATE
```

and the structure of STOCK-RECORD described as:

```
01   STOCK-RECORD
     02   PART-NO
     02   QTY
          03   OLD-STOCK
          03   NEW-STOCK
     02   PRICE
```

The numbers 01, 02 and 03 are *level numbers*. These numbers are used to show the relationships of the fields in the record, namely the level structure. The record name is always given the level number 01. Then, in the above examples, the first subdivision has the level number 02 and the next subdivision has the level number 03.

The 01 level number must start in Area A, and all other entries must be within Area B (see Appendix 1, rules 1e and 2c). Usually 02 level entries start at column 12, and any further subdivisions are indented to make the structure more obvious.

In the next record DD, MM, and YY stand for day, month, and year:

STUDENT-RECORD				
NAME	ENROLMENT-DATE			CLASS
	DD	MM	YY	

◐ Qu 5.1 Write Data Division entries to show the level structure of the above record.

So far we have used level numbers 01, 02 and 03. However, any number up to 49 can be used (more than is ever needed) and they need not be consecutive. The record name must always have the 01 level number, but the first subdivision could be 03 and the next 05 and so on. So the level structure of STOCK-RECORD could be shown as:

```
01   STOCK-RECORD
     03   PART-NO
     03   QTY
          05   OLD-STOCK
          05   NEW-STOCK
     03   PRICE
```

Subdivision fields must be given higher level numbers than the field to which they relate.

The use of 01, 03, 05, 07 etc. (or even 01, 05, 10, 15) allow for insertions in the record if necessary. However, in this book we will use consecutive level numbers 01, 02, 03, 04 etc.

In a record, fields that are sub-divided are called *group* fields; fields that are not subdivided are called *elementary* fields. In the stock record above, the group fields are STOCK-RECORD and QTY; the elementary fields are PART-NO, OLD-STOCK, NEW-STOCK and PRICE.

Note that the 01 level entry, the record name, is itself a field. Indeed it is possible to have a record consisting of only one field with no sub-divisions, for example:

      01   PRINT-RECORD

◐ **Qu 5.2** In the student record described in Qu 5.1 identify (a) the group fields, (b) the elementary fields.

Now we will add picture clauses to give full record descriptions. Only elementary fields are given picture clauses, not group fields. So in the next example, CUSTOMER-RECORD and ADDRESS do not have picture clauses since they are group fields:

```
        01   CUSTOMER-RECORD.
            02   NAME             PIC X(20).
            02   ADDRESS.
                03    STREET       PIC X(20).
                03    TOWN         PIC X(20).
                03    POST-CODE    PIC X(8).
            02   ORDER-VALUE      PIC 9(6).
```

Ans 5.1 01 STUDENT-RECORD
            02 NAME
            02 ENROLMENT-DATE
                03 DD
                03 MM
                03 YY
            02 CLASS

A group field is always taken to be alphanumeric, and its size is determined by the elementary fields it contains. So the size of CUSTOMER-RECORD is 74 characters.

◐ Qu 5.3 What is the size of the ADDRESS field in the customer record above?

A final rule about record descriptions is that each field description entry must be followed by a full stop, including those for group fields. So in the customer record above, CUSTOMER-RECORD and ADDRESS are both followed by full stops.

The structure of an order record is shown below, with the sizes of the elementary fields given in brackets. We have abbreviated RECORD to REC, and CUSTOMER to CUST.

ORDER-REC					
DATE			CUST-NAME (20)	ORDER	
DD (2)	MM (2)	YY (2)		ITEM (6)	QTY (5)

◐ Qu 5.4 Write a complete description for the above record, given that QTY is numeric and all other fields are alphanumeric.

Note: With some systems, DATE is a reserved word. So you may need to change DATE to ORDER-DATE or O-DATE.

Ans 5.2 (a) STUDENT-RECORD and ENROLMENT-DATE
       (b) NAME, DD, MM, YY and CLASS

Displaying and accepting records

In Units 1 and 2, we discussed displaying individual fields on the screen and accepting fields from the screen. The same procedures can be applied to complete records.

Suppose that in the following record:

```
01   STOCK-REC.
     02   ITEM-NO    PIC X(6).
     02   QTY        PIC 9(4).
```

the contents of ITEM-NO is 446210 and of QTY is 0500. Then the statement:

DISPLAY STOCK REC.

will give the following display on the screen:

4462100500

This is not very readable, so we need to insert spaces between the fields. Spaces are inserted in records by using special fields called FILLER fields. For example:

```
01   STOCK-REC.
     02   ITEM-NO    PIC X(6).
     02   FILLER     PIC X(5).
     02   QTY        PIC 9(4).
```

Now provided the FILLER field contains spaces, the DISPLAY statement will output:

46210   0500

with five spaces between the fields.

FILLER fields are used to insert spaces in records and are always alphanumeric in type. The stock record in the Data Division shown on page 58 contains two FILLER fields, which separate the other fields by four spaces.

Now consider this record:

```
01   CAR-REC.
     02   REG-NO    PIC X(7).
     02   OWNER     PIC X(20).
```

◐ Qu 5.5 Amend the above record so the fields can be separated by ten spaces when it is displayed on the screen.

When accepting input into a record from the screen, the FILLER fields play an important role in cursor control in CIS COBOL. As you type in values and reach the end of a field, the cursor automatically jumps to the beginning of the next non-FILLER field.

For example, assume STOCK-REC has been defined with a FILLER field as shown on page 56, and a program is now executing the statement:

ACCEPT STOCK-REC AT 0110.

If you now type say 66744A, the cursor will automatically jump five spaces and you can then type the quantity. When you have typed entries for all fields in a record, you press RETURN to accept the whole record.

The action of the cursor control keys is normally as follows in CIS COBOL:

→   move forward one character position

←   move back one position
    OR if at the beginning of a field, jump back to the last non-FILLER field

↓   jump forward to the next non-FILLER field

↑   jump back to the last non-FILLER field

Ans 5.3   48 characters

Ans 5.4
```
01   ORDER-REC.
     02   DATE.
          03   DD          PIC X(2).
          03   MM          PIC X(2).
          03   YY          PIC X(2).
     02   CUST-NAME        PIC X(20).
     02   ORDER.
          03   ITEM        PIC X(6).
          03   QTY         PIC 9(5).
```

You can move backwards and forwards between fields at any time before pressing RETURN; entries are not accepted by the program until you press RETURN. You cannot type into FILLER fields.

The ↓ key is particularly useful with alphanumeric fields. For example, suppose a PIC X(20) field is used to accept customer names and you type in JONES. You can then either type 15 spaces (to reach the end of the field) or simply press the ↓ key. Both actions will take you to the start of the next non-FILLER field.

◐ Qu 5.6 In the program below, assume that the ACCEPT STOCK-REC statement is being executed. If you type PAPER CLIPS into the DESCRIPTION field and then press the ↓ key, how many spaces will the cursor jump?

Note that this action of FILLER fields in records input from the screen is not available in all versions of COBOL.

When you have access to a computer, you could try out the effects of FILLER fields by running a program like the following:

```
DATA DIVISION.
WORKING-STORAGE SECTION.
01    STOCK-REC.
      02    ITEM-NO          PIC X(6).
      02    FILLER           PIC X(4).
      02    DESCRIPTION      PIC X(15).
      02    FILLER           PIC X(4).
      02    QTY              PIC 9(4).
01    ANS                    PIC X.

PROCEDURE DIVISION.
      MOVE SPACE TO ANS.
      PERFORM LOOP UNTIL ANS = "N".
      STOP RUN.
LOOP.
      DISPLAY SPACE UPON CRT.
      MOVE SPACE TO STOCK-REC.
      ACCEPT STOCK-REC AT 0110.
      SUBTRACT 1 FROM QTY.
      DISPLAY STOCK-REC AT 0310.
*end of data?
      DISPLAY "Another record? Y/N" AT 0510.
      ACCEPT ANS AT 0531.
```

Note that in this program, the statement:

   MOVE SPACE TO STOCK-REC.

ensures the FILLER fields contain spaces, and also clears out the current values in the non-FILLER fields (which may not be overwritten by new screen entries).

Incidentally, it is always possible to move SPACE to a record, even when it contains numeric elementary fields. The record is itself a group field and is therefore alphanumeric (see page 55).

◐ Qu 5.7 Suppose the above program is running and the cursor is at the beginning of the first line. You now: type 1234-B, type STAPLES, press ↓ , type 0075, and press RETURN. What is then displayed on the third line? Show spaces by the △ symbol.

For simplicity, in Units 6 and 7 we will accept fields in records separately rather than accepting the record as a whole. However, we will return to accepting records as a whole from the screen in Unit 8 (page 102).

Ans 5.5 01   CAR-REC.
              02   REG-NO   PIC X(7).
              02   FILLER   PIC X(10).
              02   OWNER   PIC X(20).

VALUE clauses

Fields defined in the Working-Storage Section can be given an initial value by a VALUE clause in the field description. For example:

    01   TOTAL   PIC 9(6)   VALUE ZERO.

This initial value could also be given by the Procedure Division statement:

    MOVE ZERO TO TOTAL.

Both entries have the same effect, but sometimes it is more convenient to give initial values in the Data Division.

Alphanumeric literals are often used in VALUE clauses, for example:

```
01    HEADING.
      02    HEAD-1    PIC X(4)     VALUE "Item".
      02    FILLER    PIC X(6)     VALUE SPACE.
      02    HEAD-2    PIC X(11)    VALUE "Description".
      02    FILLER    PIC X(8)     VALUE SPACE.
      02    HEAD-3    PIC X(8)     VALUE "Quantity".
```

Now the statement:

    DISPLAY HEADING AT 0110.

will display the following heading:

    Item   Description   Quantity

with six spaces after "Item" and eight spaces after "Description". (This heading could be used in the program on page 58.)

When using a printer, headings are often set up in working storage like this. However, with screen displays it can be easier to include literals in DISPLAY statements (with the AT option) when setting up headings and field labels (for example see Exercise D, page 104).

Ans 5.6   Eight spaces

Up to now we have assigned initial values to fields using MOVE statements as, for example, in the Procedure Division on page 35. For similar purposes in future programs, we will assign initial values using the VALUE clause as, for example, in the program on page 77.

◐ Qu 5.8 In the program on page 77, state the initial value of the fields (a) YES and (b) EOF.

◐ Qu 5.9 An aircraft reservations program uses the field SEATS for seats available. Write a field description that gives SEATS an initial value of 152 (the capacity of the aircraft). Use the 02 level number.

Note: In the next Unit you will see that fields can be declared in another section of the Data Division, called the File Section. VALUE clauses cannot be used in the File Section, they can be used only in the Working-Storage Section.

Ans 5.7   1234-B△△△△ STAPLES△△△△△△△△△△△ 0074

Summary (Unit 5)

- A more complete format for field descriptions than given in Unit 4 is:

  level-number $\begin{Bmatrix} \underline{\text{data-name}} \\ \text{FILLER} \end{Bmatrix}$ [$\underline{\text{PIC}}$ picture]   [$\underline{\text{VALUE}}$ IS literal]

- A record is a group of related fields. Some fields may be subdivisions of other fields. Fields that are subdivided are called group fields; fields that are not subdivided are elementary fields.

- The record name takes the level number 01. In this book the first level of subdivision takes the level number 02, the next level takes 03, and so on. Only elementary fields have picture clauses.

- The 01 level number must start in Area A. All other entries must be within Area B. Each field description must end with a full stop.

- FILLER fields can be used to insert spaces in records. On input from the screen, the cursor jumps over FILLER fields in records in CIS COBOL.

- The VALUE clause can be used to give a field an initial value in the Working-Storage Section only.

Further questions

5.10 Identify any errors in the following Data Division (there are no layout errors):

```
DATA DIVISION.
WORKING STORAGE SECTION.
01    MILES-REC
      02    INITIAL-MILES    PIC 9(6).
      02    FILLER           PIC X(4).
      02    FINAL-MILES      PIC 9(6).
01    MILES-DRIVEN           PIC 9(6).
01    CHARGE                 PIC 9(7).
```

5.11 Using the above Data Division, write a Procedure Division that will display the car hire charge when the user types in the initial and final mileages. Use a rate of 20 pence a mile. Do not include text or use a loop.

5.12 Write a program to convert hours and minutes into minutes. Use a record called TIME that contains fields called HRS and MINS, and use a field called STORE to store the number of minutes. Between accepting hours and minutes, the cursor should jump one space. Assume hours will be less than 100. Do not include text or use a loop.

Ans 5.8 (a) 0   (b) one space

Ans 5.9   02   SEATS   PIC 9(3)   VALUE 152.

Unit 6 Sequential files

Up to now, all input and output has been from and to the screen. However, other devices can be used, including disk drives, tape drives and printers. These devices allow data to be stored permanently, whereas data output to a screen is held only temporarily. When using devices other than the screen, data is organized into *files*.

In COBOL, a file is a series of similar records input from or output to disk, tape or a printer (in the past, punched cards and paper tape were used, but these are now generally obsolete). With microcomputers, disk and printers are normally used. Files stored on disk are called disk files; files output to a printer are called print files.

COBOL was originally developed for handling large data files, and has powerful file handling facilities. Different types of file can be used. In this Unit we look at *sequential* files, where each record in the file can be accessed in sequence only. Later we look at *random* files, where each record can be accessed at random as well as in sequence.

Data Division entries

Files must be defined in the Data Division (like records and fields). A minimum general format is simply:

>   FD   file-name

where FD stands for file description, and the rules for file-names are the same as for data-names (page 11).

We have said that a file is a series of related records. After the file description comes a record description, which defines the records that make up the file. For example, suppose a file called AGE-FILE contains records called AGE-REC, we could write:

```
FD  AGE-FILE.
01  AGE-REC.
    02  AGE     PIC 99.
    02  NAME    PIC X(20).
```

File descriptions appear in the File Section of the Data Division (not the Working-Storage Section). Below is a complete Data Division that defines a file called STOCK-FILE, which contains records called STOCK-REC:

```
DATA DIVISION.
FILE SECTION.
FD  STOCK-FILE.
01  STOCK-REC.
    02  PART-NO   PIC X(6).
    02  QTY       PIC 9(6).
```

The letters FD must start in Area A, and the file-name must be in Area B (see Appendix 1); the whole entry must end with a full stop. Several other clauses can appear in the file description, but these are all optional in CIS COBOL and we will not use them. However, we should mention one clause that is mandatory in several COBOL versions. The general format is:

$$\underline{\text{LABEL}}\ \underline{\text{RECORDS}} \left\{ \begin{matrix} \underline{\text{STANDARD}} \\ \underline{\text{OMITTED}} \end{matrix} \right\}$$

and it gives information on labels that may appear at the beginning and end of a file. Refer to the reference manual for your system for more details.

◐ Qu 6.1 A program uses a file called CAR-FILE, which contains records called CAR-REC as defined on page 57. Write a Data Division that defines the file.

Procedure Division entries for input

We turn now to statements in the Procedure Division that allow data to be input from a file (we deal with output to a file later).

Before a file can be used, it must be opened using an OPEN statement. If a file already exists and we want to input data from it, the format of the OPEN statement is:

>   OPEN INPUT file-name

After using a file, it must be closed using a CLOSE statement. The general format is:

>   CLOSE file-name

There is no need to include the word INPUT when closing a file.

◐ Qu 6.2 A stock control program is to input data from the file defined in the Data Division on page 65. Write statements that will (a) open the file, (b) close the file.

After opening, data can be input from the file. In this Unit we are considering sequential files, where each record is input in sequence. To input records from a sequential file, we use a READ statement with the following format:

>   READ file-name AT END imperative-statement . . .

where an imperative statement is one that is not conditional, and hence excludes IF statements. Here is an example:

>   READ AGE-FILE AT END MOVE "E" TO EOF.

On the first execution of this statement, the first record in AGE-FILE is read. On the second execution, the second record is read and so on. When the end of the file is reached, the statement following AT END is executed. So here a field called EOF (standing for end of file) is given the value E at the end of the file. EOF is simply a PIC X field used to mark reaching the end of the file; before the end of file, EOF would contain another character such as a space.

We now show a complete Procedure Division that processes the sequential file AGE-FILE (as defined on page 65):

```
PROCEDURE DIVISION.
    OPEN INPUT AGE-FILE.
    READ AGE-FILE AT END MOVE "E" TO EOF.
    PERFORM AGE-TEST UNTIL EOF = "E".
    CLOSE AGE-FILE.
    STOP RUN.
AGE-TEST.
    IF AGE > 45 DISPLAY NAME.
    READ AGE-FILE AT END MOVE "E" TO EOF.
```

Notice the program contains two READ statements. You may like to think why this is so (the answer is on page 70).

◐ Qu 6.3   Assume AGE-FILE contains records with the following values: 51SMITH, 41BROWN, 45JONES, 46GREENE. What is displayed on the screen when a program with the above Procedure Division is run?

◐ Qu 6.4   A stock control program uses the sequential file defined in the Data Division on page 65. Write a statement that will input records from the file and give a field called EOF the value E when the end of the file is reached.

In addition to AGE-REC, the above Procedure Division uses a field called EOF. This field would be defined in the Working-Storage Section of the Data Division. The File Section is used to define only files and records contained in files. The Working-Storage Section is used for records and fields that are not part of files — in effect providing temporary 'working' storage for values held only during the program run.

```
Ans 6.1   DATA DIVISION.
          FILE SECTION.
          FD   CAR-FILE.
          01   CAR-REC.
               02   REG-NO    PIC X(7).
               02   OWNER     PIC X(20).
```

When a Data Division contains both a File Section and a Working-Storage Section, the File Section comes first (for example, see the complete program on page 77).

◐ Qu 6.5   Write a complete Data Division for the above Procedure Division. Give EOF an initial value of a space (using a VALUE clause).

If you are familiar with the READ and DATA statements in BASIC, you may have noticed similarities with the READ statement in COBOL. Although BASIC does not provide a formal record structure, the group of variables specified in a READ statement could be regarded as a record in a sequential file.

Environment Division entries

Up to this Unit, Environment Division entries have not been required for CIS COBOL, although some other COBOL versions require entries given in Appendix 2. However, when using files, all versions require Environment Division entries.

One purpose of these entries is to define the input-output devices used for files. This is done by a SELECT clause, which has the following minimal general format:

SELECT file-name ASSIGN TO implementor-name

where the form of implementor-name is specified by the designer or 'implementor' of the COBOL version being used. This name is used to define the input or output device used by the file.

For example, in some systems you can simply write clauses like:

SELECT CUST-FILE ASSIGN TO DISK.
SELECT LIST-FILE ASSIGN TO PRINTER.

showing that CUST-FILE is a disk file and LIST-FILE is a print file.

Ans 6.2   (a) OPEN INPUT STOCK-FILE.
          (b) CLOSE STOCK-FILE.

In CIS COBOL, the implementor-name for a printer is :LP: (LP stands for line printer). So the SELECT clause for LIST-FILE would be:

    SELECT LIST-FILE ASSIGN TO ":LP:".

Notice the double quotes around :LP:.

For disk files in CIS COBOL, we have to specify the file-name that the computer's operating system (CP/M) will use to identify the file on disk (see Appendix 2, pages 111–112). This is called the *external* file-name, as opposed to the *internal* file-name which we have used up to now within a program. Suppose we use an external file-name of CUST.DAT (standing for customer data, again see pages 111–112 for the form of external file-names). Then we can write:

    SELECT CUST-FILE ASSIGN TO "CUST.DAT".

again enclosing the external file-name in double quotes.

The SELECT clause appears in the Input-Output Section of the Environment Division, in a paragraph called FILE-CONTROL. Each file has its own SELECT clause. So a general model for Environment Division entries for disk and print files in CIS COBOL is:

    ENVIRONMENT DIVISION.
    INPUT-OUTPUT SECTION.
    FILE-CONTROL.
        SELECT disk-file-name   ASSIGN TO   "external-file-name".
        SELECT print-file-name ASSIGN TO   ":LP:".

The SELECT clause must be in Area B and must end with a full stop. Note the hyphens in INPUT-OUTPUT and FILE-CONTROL.

The SELECT clause is also used to specify the type of file (e.g. sequential or random) as we will see in the next Unit. If no type is specified, a sequential file is assumed by default.

◐   Qu 6.6   A CIS COBOL program uses a disk file called IN-FILE and a print file called OUT-FILE. Write an Environment Division, assuming the disk file has an external file-name of IN.DAT.

Ans 6.3 SMITH
          GREENE

Ans 6.4 READ STOCK-FILE AT END MOVE "E" TO EOF.

We can now give the complete program for processing AGE-FILE (containing the Procedure Division on page 67). We are using an external file-name called AGE.DAT.

```
ENVIRONMENT DIVISION.
INPUT-OUTPUT SECTION.
FILE-CONTROL.
    SELECT AGE-FILE ASSIGN TO "AGE.DAT".

DATA DIVISION.
FILE SECTION.
FD  AGE-FILE.
01  AGE-REC.
    02  AGE     PIC 99.
    02  NAME    PIC X(20).
WORKING-STORAGE SECTION.
01  EOF         PIC X       VALUE SPACE.

PROCEDURE DIVISION.
    OPEN INPUT AGE-FILE.
    READ AGE-FILE AT END MOVE "E" TO EOF.
    PERFORM AGE-TEST UNTIL EOF = "E".
    CLOSE AGE-FILE.
    STOP RUN.
AGE-TEST.
    IF AGE > 45 DISPLAY NAME.
    READ AGE-FILE AT END MOVE "E" TO EOF.
```

We will now answer the question: why have two READ statements? At first sight, the obvious procedure might be to omit the first READ statement and write the AGE-TEST paragraph as:

```
AGE-TEST.
    READ AGE-FILE AT END MOVE "E" TO EOF.
    IF AGE > 45 DISPLAY NAME.
```

The problem here is that the end of the AGE-TEST paragraph must be reached before the PERFORM statement tests for the value of EOF. This could mean the last record being processed twice (e.g. with records as given in Qu 6.3, the name GREENE would be displayed twice). We place a READ statement at the end of a data input loop so that the program breaks out of the loop *immediately* the end of file is detected.

Ans 6.5   See the Data Division above

Procedure Division entries for output

To create a new file and output data to it, we use an OPEN statement with the following format:

>   OPEN OUTPUT file-name

This creates a new empty file. If a file with the specified name already exists on the disk being used by the program, that file is deleted (and the data lost).

After using the file, it must be closed using a CLOSE statement. The general format is as shown on page 66.

Of course, you cannot yet run the above program because AGE-FILE does not exist. In the next section, we will create this file.

◐ Qu 6.7   A stock control program is to output data to a new file defined in the Data Division on page 65. Write statements that will (a) open the file, (b) close the file.

After opening, data can be output to the file. To output records to a sequential file, we use a WRITE statement with the following format:

>   WRITE record-name

Notice that we read a file-name, but write a record-name. Of course, in the WRITE statement, the record specified belongs to the file we want to write to. So to write a record to AGE-FILE, we use the statement:

>   WRITE AGE-REC.

Ans 6.6   ENVIRONMENT DIVISION.
          INPUT-OUTPUT SECTION.
          FILE-CONTROL.
              SELECT IN-FILE ASSIGN TO "IN.DAT".
              SELECT OUT-FILE ASSIGN TO ":LP:".

Below is a complete Procedure Division for creating and inputting data into AGE-FILE:

```
PROCEDURE DIVISION.
    OPEN OUTPUT AGE-FILE.
    PERFORM DATA-IN UNTIL ANS = "N".
    CLOSE AGE-FILE.
    STOP RUN.
DATA-IN.
    DISPLAY SPACE UPON CRT.
    MOVE SPACE TO AGE-REC.
    DISPLAY "Type name" AT 0110.
    ACCEPT NAME AT 0121.
    DISPLAY "Type age" AT 0310.
    ACCEPT AGE AT 0320.
    WRITE AGE-REC.
*more data?
    DISPLAY "Another record?  Y/N" AT 0510.
    ACCEPT ANS AT 0531.
```

◐ Qu 6.8   Write a Data Division for a program with the above Procedure Division. Give ANS an initial value of a space.

◐ Qu 6.9   A stock control program uses the sequential file defined in the Data Division on page 65. Write a statement that will output a record to the file.

OPEN and CLOSE statements

We can now give the full general format of the OPEN statement:

$$\underline{\text{OPEN}} \left\{ \left\{ \begin{array}{l} \underline{\text{INPUT}} \\ \underline{\text{OUTPUT}} \\ \underline{\text{EXTEND}} \\ \underline{\text{I-O}} \end{array} \right\} \text{file-name} \ldots \right\} \ldots$$

where file-names can be separated by commas. So, for example, we can write:

```
OPEN INPUT    OLD-FILE
     OUTPUT NEW FILE, PRINT-FILE.
```

The options are as follows:

> INPUT   allows input from a file
> OUTPUT allows output to a new file
> EXTEND allows output to an existing file
> I-O   allows input from and output to a file

We have already discussed the INPUT and OUTPUT options. INPUT opens an existing file for reading from. OUTPUT creates a new empty file for writing to; if a file with the specified name already exists on the disk being used by the program, that file is deleted (and the data lost).

To add records to an existing file, we must use the EXTEND option rather than the OUTPUT option. For example:

> OPEN EXTEND AGE-FILE.

will allow a program to write further records to AGE-FILE. The EXTEND option is similar to the OUTPUT option but does not delete the existing records.

The I-O option (standing for Input-Output) allows a program to both read and write to a file. This option is discussed in the next Unit (noting that a sequential file must be open for I-O when using a REWRITE statement, see page 84).

The format of the CLOSE statement is:

> <u>CLOSE</u> file-name . . .

irrespective of how the file is opened. File-names can be separated by commas.

◐   Qu 6.10   Write three OPEN statements that will: (a) create a new file called MY-FILE, (b) allow records to be written to an existing file called MY-FILE, (c) allow records to be read from a file called MY-FILE.

Ans 6.7   (a) OPEN OUTPUT STOCK-FILE.
         (b) CLOSE STOCK-FILE.

Summary (Unit 6)

○ A file is a series of similar records stored using a device such as a disk or tape drive, or output to a printer. In *sequential* files, records can be accessed in sequence only.

○ The device used must be specified in the Environment Division using a SELECT clause with the minimum format:

SELECT file-name ASSIGN TO implementor-name

In CIS COBOL the implementor-name forms are:
          for disk files: "external-file-name"
          for print files: ":LP:"

○ The SELECT clause occurs in the Input-Output Section of the Environment Division, in a paragraph called FILE-CONTROL. The clause must be in Area B and end with a full stop.

○ A file must be defined in the File Section of the Data Division. The format is:

FD file-name

where FD stands for file description. This entry is followed by a description of the records in the file.

○ In the Procedure Division, a file must be opened before use and closed after use. The formats of the OPEN and CLOSE statements are given on pages 72 and 73.

○ Records are input from a file using a READ statement and output to a file using a WRITE statement. Formats for sequential files are:

READ file-name AT END imperative-statement . . .

WRITE record-name

A READ statement must end with a full stop, but there must be no full stop within the statement.

Ans 6.8   See page 75.

Ans 6.9   WRITE STOCK-REC.

Further questions

6.11 A program processes a sequential file called CUSTOMER-FILE that contains records with the description shown at the bottom of page 54. The file is held on disk with an external file-name of CUST.DAT. The program uses a field called EOF for detecting the end of the file (with an initial value of a space). Write Environment and Data Divisions.

6.12 For the program in Qu 6.11, write a Procedure Division that will display the names of all customers living in BRIGHTON. Use a paragraph called TOWN-TEST.

Ans 6.8 DATA DIVISION.
FILE SECTION.
FD   AGE-FILE.
01   AGE-REC.
      02   AGE   PIC 99.
      02   NAME   PIC X(20).
WORKING-STORAGE SECTION.
01   ANS   PIC X   VALUE SPACE.

Ans 6.10 (a) OPEN OUTPUT MY-FILE.
         (b) OPEN EXTEND MY-FILE.
         (c) OPEN INPUT MY-FILE.

Exercise B

The program below illustrates the analysis of questionnaires or census data. The program analyses one question, which can have replies of yes (Y), no (N) or don't know (D).

We have used the data-name NOE rather than NO for the total of negative replies because NO is a reserved word in some COBOL versions.

In the Working-Storage Section, we have grouped the total fields into a record called TOTALS. This is done simply to make the program more readable (we could have used a separate 01 field for each total). TOTAL is never used as a complete record in the Procedure Division.

We have tested for any empty file in the Procedure Division. If the file contains no records, the run stops immediately.

The statements in the YES-REPLIES and NO-REPLIES paragraphs could have been included in the ANALYSIS paragraph in this short program. But as programs get longer, this type of breakdown becomes more necessary, and is typical of structured approaches to programming (see page 107).

Examples of values for the DATA-REC records are:

```
YM41
NF30
DM24
YM24
```

Now answer these questions:

(a) Suppose the program is running and has already read hundreds of records. The totals accumulated so far are YES 1550, NOE 1261, YES-MALE 0735, and YES-OV-40 1170. The first of the four example records above is about to be read. Assuming that these are the last four records in the file, what is displayed after the last record is read?

(b) Modify the program so that it will also display the total under age 25 answering no. (Use a field called NO-UN-25.)

(c) Modify the program so that it will display the total number of people who answered the question. (Use a field called TOT-REPLIES.)

```
ENVIRONMENT DIVISION.
INPUT-OUTPUT SECTION.
FILE-CONTROL.
    SELECT DATA-FILE ASSIGN TO "QUEST.DAT".
```

```
DATA DIVISION.
FILE SECTION.
FD   DATA-FILE.
01   DATA-REC.
     02   REPLY      PIC X.
     02   SEX        PIC X.
     02   AGE        PIC 99.
WORKING-STORAGE SECTION.
01   TOTALS.
     02   YES        PIC 9(4)    VALUE ZERO.
     02   NOE        PIC 9(4)    VALUE ZERO.
     02   YES-MALE   PIC 9(4)    VALUE ZERO.
     02   YES-OV-40  PIC 9(4)    VALUE ZERO.
01   EOF             PIC X       VALUE SPACE.

PROCEDURE DIVISION.
     OPEN INPUT DATA-FILE.
     READ DATA-FILE AT END
         DISPLAY "FILE EMPTY"
         CLOSE DATA-FILE
         STOP RUN.
     PERFORM ANALYSIS UNTIL EOF = "E".
     PERFORM DISPLAY-RESULTS.
     CLOSE DATA-FILE.
     STOP RUN.
ANALYSIS.
     IF REPLY = "Y"   PERFORM YES-REPLIES.
     IF REPLY = "N"   PERFORM NO-REPLIES.
     READ DATA-FILE AT END MOVE "E" TO EOF.
YES-REPLIES.
     ADD 1 TO YES.
     IF SEX = "M" ADD 1 TO YES-MALE.
     IF AGE > 40   ADD 1 TO YES-OV-40.
NO-REPLIES.
     ADD 1 TO NOE.
DISPLAY-RESULTS.
     DISPLAY SPACE UPON CRT.
     DISPLAY "Total answering Yes"              AT 0110.
     DISPLAY "Total answering No"               AT 0210.
     DISPLAY "Total of males answering Yes"     AT 0410.
     DISPLAY "Total over age 40 answering Yes"  AT 0510.
     DISPLAY YES          AT 0143.
     DISPLAY NOE          AT 0243.
     DISPLAY YES-MALE     AT 0443.
     DISPLAY YES-OV-40    AT 0543.
```

Unit 7 Indexed files

In the last Unit we looked at sequential files, where records are accessed in sequence only. In this Unit we look at *random* files, where records can be accessed at random as well as in sequence in a sequential file, records are accessed in the physical order in which they are stored: the first record, then the second, then the third, and so on. So to access, say, the 200th record, the program would have to read through the previous 199 records first. In a random file, the program can directly access any particular record.

One type of random file in COBOL is the *indexed* file (sometimes called the indexed sequential access method or ISAM file). This type of file contains an index that shows the position of each record in the file. The program can use this index to find any particular record.

With an indexed file, the SELECT clause in the Environment Division must include an ORGANIZATION entry. For example:

```
SELECT STOCK-FILE ASSIGN TO "STOCK.DAT"
    ORGANIZATION IS INDEXED
```

This entry specifies an indexed file (on disk) called STOCK-FILE. The word ORGANIZATION must be spelt with a Z. The indentation is for clarity only.

An indexed file can be accessed sequentially or randomly. If random access is used, an ACCESS entry must be added (after the ORGANIZATION entry):

```
ACCESS IS RANDOM
```

With random access, yet another entry must be added showing how particular records are to be identified. This involves specifying that one field in the record is to be the *key* field for identifying particular records. Typical key fields are part number (or name), or customer number (or name). For example, in the following record we could use PART-NO or NAME as the key field:

```
01    STOCK-REC.
      02    PART-NO    PIC X(6).
      02    NAME       PIC X(12).
      02    QTY        PIC 9(6).
```

Suppose we use PART-NO as the key field. Then we add a RECORD KEY entry to the SELECT clause:

```
SELECT STOCK-FILE ASSIGN TO "STOCK.DAT"
    ORGANIZATION IS INDEXED
    ACCESS IS RANDOM
    RECORD KEY IS PART-NO.    ← (key field specified)
```

Note that there are no full stops within the SELECT clause, but there is one at the end.

Random files are always stored on disk. It is not possible to randomly access records on tape.

◐ **Qu 7.1** Write a SELECT clause for an indexed file called MEMBERS that is to be accessed randomly using a key field called MEM-NO. The external file-name is MEM.DAT.

Accessing a record   A particular record in an indexed file can be accessed using a READ statement. The format is:

<u>READ</u> file-name <u>INVALID</u> KEY statement . . .

where the statement following INVALID KEY is executed if a record with the specified key does not exist. For example:

READ STOCK-FILE INVALID KEY MOVE "U" TO FLAG.

where FLAG is a PIC X field used to record the success of the read. The letter U here stands for unsuccessful (the field would be initialized with a space value, or perhaps S for successful).

Suppose that at the time the above READ statement is executed, the value of PART-NO is 1212. The program will attempt to access the record with part number 1212. If this record does not exist, then FLAG will be given the value of U.

The following sequence will access a particular stock record and display the quantity in stock:

```
READ STOCK-FILE INVALID KEY MOVE "U" TO FLAG.
IF FLAG = "U"
    DISPLAY "Record not found"
ELSE
    DISPLAY "Quantity in stock   ", QTY.
```

Note that for simplicity in this Unit, we will not use the AT option in ACCEPT and DISPLAY statements (but note the possible effects of this on pages 36 and 37). However, we do use the AT option in Exercise C, which combines all the random actions on indexed files in this Unit (page 92).

◐ Qu 7.2 Write a sequence that will access a record in the MEMBERS file specified in Qu 7.1. Display the subscription due from the member (held in a field called SUB). If the record does not exist, display NO SUCH MEMBER. Use a field called FLAG as in the above sequence.

Before a random file can be read, the key field must be set to identify the required record. So before the READ statement in the above sequence, there will be statements such as:

```
DISPLAY "Type the part number of the required record".
ACCEPT PART-NO.
```

On the opposite page is a complete program for accessing a particular record in STOCK-FILE (this program will access only one record — we will set up a loop for multiple accesses in Exercise C). Notice that, as when reading a sequential file, an indexed file is opened for INPUT (see page 66).

◐ Qu 7.3 In the opposite program, suppose a user types 1234A in reply to the WHICH PART NUMBER? prompt. What is the value of FLAG at the end of the program if the record with part number 1234A (a) exists, and (b) does not exist.

```
ENVIRONMENT DIVISION.
INPUT-OUTPUT SECTION.
FILE-CONTROL.
    SELECT STOCK-FILE ASSIGN TO "STOCK.DAT"
        ORGANIZATION IS INDEXED
        ACCESS IS RANDOM
        RECORD KEY IS PART-NO.    ← key field specified

DATA DIVISION.
FILE SECTION.
FD  STOCK-FILE.
01  STOCK-REC.
    02  PART-NO     PIC X(4).    ← key field
    02  QTY         PIC 9(6).
WORKING-STORAGE SECTION.
01  FLAG            PIC X    VALUE "S".

PROCEDURE DIVISION.
    OPEN INPUT STOCK-FILE.
    PERFORM INQUIRY.
    CLOSE STOCK-FILE.
    STOP RUN.
INQUIRY.
    MOVE SPACE TO PART-NO.
    DISPLAY "Which part number?".
    ACCEPT PART-NO.    ← key field set
    READ STOCK-FILE INVALID KEY MOVE "U" TO FLAG.
    IF FLAG = "U"
        DISPLAY "No such record"
    ELSE
        DISPLAY "Quantity in stock   ", QTY.
```

Ans 7.1 SELECT MEMBERS ASSIGN TO "MEM.DAT"
            ORGANIZATION IS INDEXED
            ACCESS IS RANDOM
            RECORD KEY IS MEM-NO.

Adding a record A record can be added to an indexed file by using a WRITE statement. The format is:

<u>WRITE</u> record-name <u>INVALID</u> KEY statement . . .

where the statement following INVALID KEY is executed if the value of the key field is duplicated. In CIS COBOL, the value of the key field in each record must be unique — two records cannot have the same key field value.

The following Procedure Division will add one record to STOCK-FILE. The Environment and Data Divisions would be the same as those on page 81 (except the FLAG field is not needed). Note that, as when writing to sequential files, an indexed file is opened for OUTPUT.

```
PROCEDURE DIVISION.
    OPEN OUTPUT STOCK-FILE.
    PERFORM ADDITION.
    CLOSE STOCK-FILE.
    STOP RUN.
ADDITION.
    MOVE SPACE TO PART-NO.
    DISPLAY "Type part number".
    ACCEPT PART-NO.
    DISPLAY "Type quantity in stock".
    ACCEPT QTY.
    WRITE STOCK-REC INVALID KEY
        DISPLAY "Duplicate part number".
```

Suppose a record with part number 123 already exists in the STOCK-FILE. If the user now attempts to add a new record with part number 123, the program will display DUPLICATE PART NUMBER and the record will not be added to the file.

◐ Qu 7.4 Write a statement that will add a record to the MEMBERS file specified in Qu 7.1. The file contains records called MEM-REC. If the membership number used already exists in the file, display MEMBERSHIP NUMBER NOT UNIQUE.

Ans 7.2 READ MEMBERS INVALID KEY MOVE "U" TO FLAG.
    IF FLAG = "U"
        DISPLAY "No such member"
    ELSE
        DISPLAY "Subscription due   ", SUB.

Updating a record   A particular record in an index file can be updated, or amended, using a REWRITE statement. The procedure is:

1 Access the record using a READ statement
2 Update the record
3 Replace the updated record using a REWRITE statement

The REWRITE statement inserts the updated record into the same physical position in the file as the original record. Thus the contents of the original record are overwritten. This procedure is sometimes called 'updating in place'.

The format of the REWRITE statement in indexed files is:

>   <u>REWRITE</u> record-name <u>INVALID</u> KEY statement . . .

where the statement following INVALID KEY is executed if the new updated record does not have the same key field value as the old record. This can happen only in the unlikely event of the programmer changing the key field value between the READ and REWRITE statements.

The file must be opened in I-O mode (standing for Input-Output). This is the last option in the OPEN statement (see page 73). The I-O mode allows input from the file (for the READ) and output to the file (for the REWRITE).

The following Procedure Division updates one record in STOCK-FILE. The Environment and Data Division would be the same as those on page 81 except for an AMOUNT field defined in the Working-Storage Section (as a PIC 9(6) field).

```
PROCEDURE DIVISION.
    OPEN I-O STOCK-FILE.
    PERFORM UPDATE.
    CLOSE STOCK-FILE.
    STOP RUN.
UPDATE.
    MOVE SPACE TO PART-NO.
    DISPLAY "Which part number?".
    ACCEPT PART-NO.
    READ STOCK-FILE INVALID KEY MOVE "U" TO FLAG.
    IF FLAG = "U"
        DISPLAY "No such record"
    ELSE
        DISPLAY "Type quantity withdrawn from stock"
        ACCEPT AMOUNT
        SUBTRACT AMOUNT FROM QTY
        REWRITE STOCK-REC INVALID KEY DISPLAY "Error".
```

In Qu 7.5 below assume a stock record holds the following values:

    PART NO   445A
    QTY   000784

◐ **Qu 7.5** Suppose a program with the above Procedure Divison is running and the user types 445A in reply to the first prompt and 000064 in reply to the second prompt. Will the record concerned be updated and, if so, what are the values in the updated record?

The REWRITE statement (without the INVALID KEY clause) can also be used with sequential files. Now each record in the file is read in turn, and then updated (if necessary) and rewritten back to the file. Updates can be entered directly from the screen, as we have done above, or held in a separate 'transaction' file. An alternative to updating in place is to create a new file (using a WRITE rather than a REWRITE statement). More comprehensive books on COBOL will contain details of sequential update techniques.

Deleting a record   A particular record in an indexed file can be deleted using a DELETE statement. The format is:

    <u>DELETE</u> file-name <u>INVALID</u> KEY statement . . .

where the statement following INVALID KEY is executed if the specified record does not exist.

There is no need to access the record first: you simply set the key field and then use the DELETE statement. The file must be open for I-O.

The following Procedure Division deletes one record from STOCK-FILE. The Environment and Data Divisions would be the same as those on page 81 (except FLAG is not needed).

Ans 7.4   WRITE MEM-REC INVALID KEY
            DISPLAY "Membership number not unique".

```
        PROCEDURE DIVISION.
            OPEN I-O STOCK-FILE.
            PERFORM DELETION.
            CLOSE STOCK-FILE.
            STOP RUN.
        DELETION.
            MOVE SPACE TO PART-NO.
            DISPLAY "Type part number for deletion".
            ACCEPT PART-NO.
            DELETE STOCK-FILE INVALID KEY DISPLAY "No such record".
```

◐ Qu 7.6 Write a paragraph called DELETION that will delete a record from the MEMBERS file specified in Qu 7.1.

A menu-driven program

We have seen examples of making a single inquiry, addition, update and deletion. A complete program would often allow all four types of transaction, and also allow multiple transactions. This is best achieved by using a menu.

A menu of options would be displayed asking the user to type, say, the letter A to make an addition or D to make a deletion. The program would then contain statements like:

```
        IF ANS = "A" PERFORM ADDITION.
        IF ANS = "D" PERFORM DELETION.
```

where the ADDITION and DELETION paragraphs would be similar to those shown on page 83 and earlier on this page.

An example of such a menu-driven program is given in Exercise C, which you may like to look at now (page 92).

Sequential access to indexed files

Before continuing, it will be helpful to give a more complete general format of the SELECT clause for sequential and indexed files:

SELECT file-name ASSIGN TO implementor-name

$$\left[\text{ORGANIZATION IS} \left\{ \begin{array}{l} \text{SEQUENTIAL} \\ \text{INDEXED} \end{array} \right\} \right]$$

$$\left[\text{ACCESS MODE IS} \left\{ \begin{array}{l} \text{SEQUENTIAL} \\ \text{RANDOM} \\ \text{DYNAMIC} \end{array} \right\} \right]$$

[RECORD KEY IS data-name]

If ORGANIZATION and ACCESS entries are omitted, SEQUENTIAL is assumed by default. The RECORD KEY entry is applicable only to indexed files. The DYNAMIC access mode will be explained later.

In Unit 6 we omitted the ORGANIZATION and ACCESS entries, so the default values were used. In the SELECT clause in the program on page 70 we could have written:

```
SELECT AGE-FILE ASSIGN TO "AGE.DAT"
    ORGANIZATION IS SEQUENTIAL
    ACCESS IS SEQUENTIAL.
```

A sequential file (i.e. ORGANIZATION SEQUENTIAL) can only be accessed sequentially. However, an indexed file (i.e. ORGANIZATION INDEXED) can be accessed sequentially or randomly. For example, for the STOCK-FILE used earlier in this Unit we could write:

```
SELECT STOCK-FILE ASSIGN TO "STOCK.DAT"
    ORGANIZATION IS INDEXED
    ACCESS IS SEQUENTIAL
    RECORD KEY IS PART-NO.
```
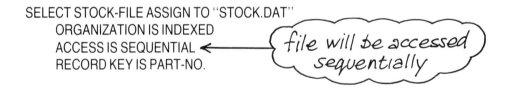

◐ Qu 7.7 Write a SELECT clause for the indexed MEMBERS file in Qu 7.1, given the file is to be accessed sequentially.

Ans 7.5 The record will be updated. The values are:
    PART-NO   445A
    QTY   000720

With sequential access, STOCK-FILE can be read like the files in Unit 6. The READ statement now accesses each record in key field sequence, not at random. The general format of the READ statement takes the AT END clause to detect the end of the file, for example:

READ STOCK-FILE AT END MOVE "E" TO EOF.

The INVALID KEY clause is not required since no record keys will be invalid.

However, the WRITE statement does require the INVALID KEY clause because records can only be added in sequence, not at random. New records must have a higher key field value than the last record in the file. For example:

WRITE STOCK-REC INVALID KEY
    DISPLAY "Record out of sequence".

If the last record in the file has a part number of 1234 and you attempt to add a record with number 1230, the INVALID KEY clause will be executed.

The REWRITE and DELETE statements (with INVALID KEY clauses) can also be used with sequential access to indexed files.

◐ Qu 7.8 State the changes needed to (a) the program on page 70 and (b) the Procedure Division on page 72 if AGE-FILE is an indexed file that is accessed sequentially. The key field is NAME.

If a file is always accessed sequentially, it is more efficient to use a sequential organization (since the index in an indexed file involves an extra overhead). But if a file is accessed randomly as well as sequentially, an indexed organization is used.

Ans 7.6 DELETION.
          MOVE SPACE TO MEM-NO.
          DISPLAY "Type membership number for deletion".
          ACCEPT MEM-NO.
          DELETE MEMBERS INVALID KEY DISPLAY "No such record".

If a file is accessed both sequentially and randomly in the same program, the access mode specified in the SELECT clause must be DYNAMIC. An example might occur in a program that randomly accesses a particular record as a starting point, and then sequentually accesses records from that point.

◐ **Qu 7.9** Write a SELECT clause for the MEMBERS file in Qu 7.1, given that the file is to be accessed sequentially and randomly in the same program.

Creating an indexed file

With CIS COBOL, you can create an indexed file using the same procedure as for adding records (pages 82 and 93). But with some other COBOL versions, you must create the file in sequential access mode with the file open for OUTPUT and with the records written in key field sequence.

To finish this Unit, two further topics on random files are mentioned:

Multikey indexed files Some COBOL versions, but not CIS COBOL, allow more than one key field with indexed files. These files can also allow duplicate key values, which is particularly useful where the key field is a name (e.g. there could be two customers called J. Smith).

Relative files A relative file is another type of random file (the SELECT clause now contains an ORGANIZATION IS RELATIVE entry). Relative files can give faster random access, but they can be more difficult to set up depending on the key field chosen. If random access time with an indexed file is too slow, a relative file might be considered.

Ans 7.7 SELECT MEMBERS ASSIGN TO "MEM.DAT"
            ORGANIZATION IS INDEXED
            ACCESS IS SEQUENTIAL
            RECORD KEY IS MEM-NO.
The third line may be omitted.

Summary (Unit 7)

○ In an indexed file, records can be accessed at random or in sequence.

○ The SELECT clause can include the following entries (the format is on page 86):

ORGANIZATION	INDEXED for indexed files, SEQUENTIAL is the default;
ACCESS	RANDOM for random access, DYNAMIC for sequential and random, SEQUENTIAL is the default;
RECORD KEY	the field for identifying records in an indexed file.

○ The following statements are used for random access to indexed files:

<u>READ</u>   file-name   INVALID KEY statement . . .
<u>WRITE</u>   record-name   INVALID KEY statement . . .
<u>REWRITE</u> record-name   INVALID KEY statement . . .
<u>DELETE</u> file-name   INVALID KEY statement . . .

The INVALID clause is executed if the record does not exist, or is duplicated, or is out of sequence as appropriate.

○ The above statements are also used for sequential access to indexed files except READ takes the AT END clause.

○ For REWRITE and DELETE statements, the file must be open for I-O. REWRITE writes a record in the same place as the last record read, and can also be used with sequential files.

Ans 7.8 (a) add to the SELECT clause (the second line may be omitted):
ORGANIZATION IS INDEXED
ACCESS IS SEQUENTIAL
RECORD KEY IS NAME.

(b) The WRITE statement becomes:
WRITE AGE-REC INVALID KEY
    DISPLAY "Record out of sequence".

Further questions

7.10 A program processes an indexed file called CAR-FILE that contains records as shown on page 57. The external file-name is CAR.DAT and the key field is REG-NO. The program uses a field called FLAG for dealing with invalid keys (with an initial value of S). Write Environment and Data Divisions.

7.11 For the program in Qu 7.10, write a paragraph called INQUIRY that will display the owner of one car with a given registration number. Do not use the AT option (see page 80).

7.12 For the program in Qu 7.10, write a paragraph called ADDITION that will add one new record to the file. Do not use the AT option (see page 80).

Ans 7.9 SELECT MEMBERS ASSIGN TO "MEM.DAT"
    ORGANIZATION IS INDEXED
    ACCESS IS DYNAMIC
    RECORD KEY IS MEM-NO.

Exercise C

The program overleaf illustrates a typical menu-driven program for processing a random file. The file records membership payments (using the STATUS field, where Y means paid and N means not paid).

Notice the invalid key flag is set to S (for successful) before a transaction to allow for cases where the flag has been set to U (for unsuccessful) in the previous transaction.

The prompt PRESS RETURN TO CONTINUE and the following ACCEPT statement prevent the screen being cleared immediately after a transaction. The prompt also in effect confirms that the transaction has been completed if there is no error message.

In the questions below, assume that the file contains the following four records:

```
1421Y
200 Y
86  Y
3344N
```

(a) What, if anything, is displayed besides the PRESS RETURN prompt after the user types the following (pressing RETURN after each entry):

1. A and then 1421 and then Y
2. A and then 1422 and then Y
3. I and then 200
4. I and then 201
5. D and then 3344
6. D and then 3345

(b) Write the UPDATE paragraph.

```
ENVIRONMENT DIVISION.
INPUT-OUTPUT SECTION.
FILE-CONTROL.
      SELECT MEMBERS ASSIGN TO "MEM.DAT"
          ORGANIZATION IS INDEXED
          ACCESS IS RANDOM
          RECORD KEY IS MEM-NO.

DATA DIVISION.
FILE SECTION.
FD    MEMBERS.
01    MEM-REC.
      02   MEM-NO       PIC X(4).
      02   STATUS       PIC X.
WORKING-STORAGE SECTION.
01    FLAG             PIC X.
01    ANS              PIC X    VALUE SPACE.

PROCEDURE DIVISION.
      OPEN I-O MEMBERS.
      PERFORM MENU UNTIL ANS = "F".
      CLOSE MEMBERS.
      STOP RUN.
MENU.
      DISPLAY SPACE UPON CRT.
      DISPLAY "A   Addition"   AT 0510.
      DISPLAY "I   Inquiry"    AT 0610.
      DISPLAY "U   Update"     AT 0710.
      DISPLAY "D   Deletion"   AT 0810.
      DISPLAY "F   Finish"     AT 0910.
      DISPLAY "Type your selection" AT 1210.
      ACCEPT ANS AT 1231.
*reset the invalid key flag
      MOVE "S" TO FLAG.
      MOVE SPACE TO MEM-REC.
      IF ANS = "A" PERFORM ADDITION.
      IF ANS = "I" PERFORM INQUIRY.
      IF ANS = "U" PERFORM UPDATE.
      IF ANS = "D" PERFORM DELETION.
```

ADDITION.
    DISPLAY SPACE UPON CRT.
    DISPLAY "Type membership number for addition" AT 0110.
    ACCEPT MEM-NO AT 0147.
    DISPLAY "Has member paid? Y/N" AT 0310.
    ACCEPT STATUS AT 0332.
    WRITE MEM-REC INVALID KEY
        DISPLAY "Duplicate membership number" AT 0610.
    DISPLAY "Press RETURN to continue" AT 1210.
    ACCEPT ANS AT 1236.

INQUIRY.
    DISPLAY SPACE UPON CRT.
    DISPLAY "Type membership number for inquiry" AT 0110.
    ACCEPT MEM-NO AT 0146.
    READ MEMBERS INVALID KEY MOVE "U" TO FLAG.
    IF FLAG = "U"
        DISPLAY "No such record" AT 0310
    ELSE
        DISPLAY "Member paid" AT 0310
        DISPLAY STATUS AT 0323
    DISPLAY "Press RETURN to continue" AT 1210.
    ACCEPT ANS AT 1236.

UPDATE.
        ⋮

DELETION.
    DISPLAY SPACE UPON CRT.
    DISPLAY "Type membership number for deletion" AT 0110.
    ACCEPT MEM-NO AT 0147.
    DELETE MEMBERS INVALID KEY
        DISPLAY "No such record" AT 0310.
    DISPLAY "Press RETURN to continue" AT 1210.
    ACCEPT ANS AT 1236.

Unit 8 Further topics

This Unit looks briefly at further topics that should be included in an elementary course, but which the beginner may wish to postpone or consider in less detail at present. Indeed, those learning COBOL mainly for interest or appreciation purposes could stop at this point. The topics include: decimal numbers, edited fields, output to a printer, and screen forms.

Decimal and signed numbers

Up to now all numeric fields have contained integer values. Now we turn to decimal values.

When a field holds a decimal value that is to be used in arithmetic, the position of the decimal point is shown by a V symbol in the picture clause. Here are some examples:

```
01    PRICE      PIC 999V99.
01    PERCENT    PICV99.
01    TOT-COST   PIC9(6)V99.
```

PRICE can hold three integer and two decimal digits; PERCENT can hold two decimal digits; and TOT-COST six integer and two decimal digits. The decimal point itself is not stored: the V symbol shows only the position of the decimal point. So PRICE is five characters long (not six) and PERCENT is two characters long.

When entering a decimal number from the screen, you may not be able to include the decimal point. For example, suppose a program is executing the statement:

```
ACCEPT PRICE.
```

where PRICE has the picture clause shown above. In CIS COBOL, to enter the value 350.45 you have to type 35045. Similarly to enter 5.99 you have to type 00599 (with the leading zeros of course).

This is not very user friendly and can lead to errors, especially with inexperienced users. So sometimes the integer and decimal digits are accepted separated (e.g. type the pounds and then the pence). Alternatively, the screen entry is accepted as an alphanumeric value, and then converted to a numeric value in the program.

With some versions of COBOL the problem has been overcome for you. Now a user could type 350.45 or 5.99 into the PRICE field and the program would automatically convert the entry to the correct form (though again the decimal point is not stored).

◐ Qu 8.1 Write picture clauses for fields that can hold (a) two integer and three decimal digits, (b) eight integer and two decimal digits.

◐ Qu 8.2 Rewrite the description for STOCK-REC on page 65 with a third field called COST, which can hold decimal numbers under 1000 with two decimal places.

If a field may hold a negative value, the field must be *signed*. This is done by placing an S in front of the picture clause. For example:

    01   BANK-BALANCE   PIC S9(6)V99.

Now if the balance is negative, the sign will be held. Again the sign itself does not take up a character position, and again some COBOL versions require special techniques for accepting negative numbers from the screen.

Edited fields

Fields that are output to the screen or a printer may be edited so that output is more easily read and understood — for example by suppressing leading zeros or by inserting decimal points, commas and currency signs. Editing is done only on fields that are displayed or printed.

We will look at two examples of editing here: suppressing leading zeros and inserting decimal points.

Zero suppression   Suppose a field is defined as follows:

    NUM   PIC 999.

and it contains 004. If NUM is displayed on the screen or output to a printer, then 004 would appear (with the two leading zeros). To suppress the leading zeros, you use the Z symbol in the picture clause:

    NUM   PIC ZZZ.

When a Z is used rather than a 9, any leading zero in that position is replaced by a blank. So now if NUM is displayed, then △△4 appears (i.e. the number 4 preceded by two blanks).

Here are some more examples:

Data	Picture	Displayed output
00015	9(5)	00015
00015	Z9(4)	△0015
00015	Z(4)9	△△△15
0600	ZZZ9	△600
0000	ZZZ9	△△△0
0000	Z(4)	△△△△ (blank)

Notice the last two examples. If the value of a field is zero and all leading zeros have been suppressed, nothing is displayed. This is undesirable, hence the last picture symbol is usually a 9 so that at least one zero digit is displayed.

Now consider these examples:

	Data	Picture
(a)	0000123	9(7)
(b)	0000123	ZZ9(5)
(c)	0000123	Z(6)9
(d)	500	ZZZ

◐ Qu 8.3 Give the displayed output for the above data and picture clauses.

◐ Qu 8.4 A field can hold six digits. Write a picture clause that will suppress any leading zeros on output, unless the value of the field is zero when one zero digit should be displayed.

Decimal point insertion In an unedited field, only the position of the decimal point is stored, not the decimal point itself. In the example below we show the implied position of the decimal point by a ∧ symbol, as in 41∧46

When a decimal point is to be displayed, it must be inserted in the picture clause:

Data	Picture	Displayed output
41∧46	99V99	4146
41∧46	99.99	41.46

The actual decimal point is always displayed at the position of the implied decimal point. If necessary, zeros are inserted so the decimal point is correctly aligned (though leading zeros can be suppressed):

Data	Picture	Displayed output
41∧46	99.9999	41.4600
41∧46	999.999	041.460
41∧46	ZZ9.999	∆41.460

Ans 8.1 (a) PIC 99V999   (b) PIC 9(8)V99

Ans 8.2 01   STOCK-REC.
              02   PART-NO   PIC X(6).
              02   QTY   PIC 9(6).
              02   COST   PIC 999V99.

Now consider these examples:

	Data	Picture
(a)	21ʌ3	99V9
(b)	21ʌ3	99.9
(c)	21ʌ3	9999.9999
(d)	21ʌ3	ZZ9.99

◐ Qu 8.5 Give the displayed output for the above data and picture clauses.

◐ Qu 8.6 A field can hold six integer and two decimal digits. Write a picture clause that will insert a decimal point on display.

Edited fields and arithmetic Edited fields cannot be used in arithmetic. So for example in the statement:

    ADD COST TO TOTAL

both COST and TOTAL must be unedited numeric fields. The question now arises: how can data be used in arithmetic and yet be displayed in an edited form? The answer is to use an unedited field for the arithmetic, and then to move the contents to an edited field for display.

For example, a program with the above ADD statement may contain the following field descriptions:

    01   TOTAL   PIC 999V99.
    01   TOTAL-E PIC ZZ9.99.

TOTAL is an unedited field for the arithmetic (the V is not an editing symbol). TOTAL-E is an edited field for display (the suffix is a useful reminder that the field is edited). We can now write:

    ADD COST TO TOTAL.
    MOVE TOTAL TO TOTAL-E.
    DISPLAY TOTAL-E.

Qu 8.7 Rewrite the program on page 42 assuming that the user will type a decimal value with two decimal places (without the decimal point). Display the output with a decimal point inserted and leading zeros suppressed using a field called NUM-E. (The answer is on page 119.)

Further editing symbols Below are listed several editing symbols, followed by an example of displayed output:

*	replace leading zeros with asterisks	****460
Z	suppress leading zeros	460
.	insert a decimal point	18.95
,	insert a comma	7,350,000
B	insert a blank	7 350 000
−	insert a minus sign (if negative)	−239
DB	insert DB (if negative)	239DB
£	insert a £ sign	£239

Multiple £ and − symbols will also suppress leading zeros, which allows a currency or negative sign to be 'floated' up to the beginning of a number. Leading asterisks are used for cheque protection.

In BASIC, some of these functions are carried out automatically, like suppressing leading zeros and inserting decimal points. Other functions would be more difficult, like floating currency signs and inserting commas.

Ans 8.3 (a) 0000123 (b) ΔΔ00123 (c) 123 (d) 500

Ans 8.4 PIC Z(5)9

Output to a printer

For printed output, a print file must be set up. In the Environment Division, a printer must be specified as the input-output device in the SELECT clause. In Unit 6 we said the implementor-name for a printer in CIS COBOL is :LP: (page 69). So to set up a print file called, say, PRINT-FILE we write:

SELECT PRINT-FILE ASSIGN TO ":LP:".

A print file can only be sequential, so there is no need for ORGANIZATION and ACCESS entries (which default to SEQUENTIAL).

In the Data Division, records are defined for the print file as usual, for example:

```
FD  PRINT-FILE.
01  PRINT-REC.
    02   NAME-P    PIC X(20).
    02   FILLER    PIC X(10).
    02   AGE-P     PIC 99.
```

We have used the P suffix to show fields belong to a print file (for reasons given shortly). FILLER fields allow spaces to be inserted, as with screen output (see page 56). Each line of a printout is regarded as a record. So when PRINT-REC is output, one line is printed starting with a person's name, followed by ten spaces (or more), and then the person's age.

In the Procedure Division, a record is output using a WRITE statement with the format:

$$\underline{\text{WRITE}} \text{ record-name } \left[\left\{\begin{array}{l}\underline{\text{BEFORE}}\\ \underline{\text{AFTER}}\end{array}\right\} \text{ADVANCING} \left\{\begin{array}{l}\text{integer[LINES]}\\ \underline{\text{PAGE}}\end{array}\right\}\right]$$

Ans 8.5   (a) 213   (b) 21.3   (c) 0021.3000   (d) 21.30

Ans 8.6   PIC 9(6).99

For example, the statement:

   WRITE PRINT-REC AFTER ADVANCING 2 LINES.

will move the paper up two lines and then print a line, so giving double spacing. The default is AFTER ADVANCING 1 LINE (you can replace LINES by LINE), giving single spacing. The option AFTER ADVANCING PAGE will start printing on a new page. Before you can write to a print file, the file must be open for OUTPUT (a printer cannot input data!).

As an example of printed output, we will modify the program on page 70. This program reads names and ages on a disk file, and displays names of people over 45 on the screen. Now suppose we want to output names and ages to a printer, rather than output names to the screen. First we insert the SELECT and FD entries for PRINT-FILE shown above. Then in the Procedure Division we insert the statements:

   OPEN OUTPUT PRINT-FILE.
   MOVE SPACE TO PRINT-REC.

and a corresponding CLOSE statement. The MOVE SPACE statement ensures the FILLER field in the record contains spaces. Lastly, the AGE-TEST paragraph becomes:

   AGE-TEST.
      IF AGE > 45
         MOVE NAME TO NAME-P
         MOVE AGE TO AGE-P
         WRITE PRINT-REC AFTER ADVANCING 3.
      READ AGE-FILE AT END MOVE "E" TO EOF.

Note that NAME-P and AGE-P are separate physical fields to NAME and AGE, so MOVE statements are required.

◐ Qu 8.8   When records are printed in the AGE-TEST paragraph above, what line spacing is used?

◐ Qu 8.9   A print file called OUT-FILE contains records called OUT-REC. Write (a) a SELECT clause for the file, (b) a statement to open the file, and (c) a statement to print a line using single spacing.

Ans 8.7   See page 119

Screen input and forms

Note: In this book a screen width of 80 characters is assumed.

For simplicity up to now, each field in a record has been accepted separately from the screen. However, a record is often accepted as a whole, which gives the user the benefit of being able to move backwards and forwards between fields (see page 57).

When accepting a record as a whole, the position of fields on the screen is specified via the record description. As an example we will accept the two fields in the Procedure Division on page 72, name and age, as a record rather than separately. The name will be accepted at position 0121 and the age at 0220. We will set up a special record for screen input called SN-REC (SN standing for screen) with fields called SN-NAME and SN-AGE:

```
01   SN-REC.
     02   FILLER      PIC X(20).
     02   SN-NAME     PIC X(20).
     02   FILLER      PIC X(59).
     02   SN-AGE      PIC 99.
```

(40+19)

The first FILLER field moves the cursor 20 spaces, so SN-NAME is accepted at position 0121. The second FILLER field moves the cursor 59 spaces: 40 spaces to the beginning of the next line and then 19 spaces to position 0220.

We can now write in the Procedure Division:

```
DISPLAY "Type name" AT 0110.
DISPLAY "Type age"  AT 0210.
ACCEPT SN-REC AT 0101.
```

We still need the AGE-REC record for writing data to AGE-FILE since storing spaces is a waste of disk space. So the next step would be to move the values in SN-REC to AGE-REC. An example of the complete procedure is given in Exercise D (p. 104).

◐ Qu 8.10 Write picture clauses for FILLER fields that will cause the cursor to move from position 0101 to (a) position 0103, (b) position 0140, (c) position 0201, (d) position 0440.

A screen with labelled fields is called a *form*. A form may contain quite a number of fields (e.g. customer number, name, address, date, items ordered, costs, etc.). The form is displayed on the screen as a whole, and the user can move between the fields using the cursor keys. In the example below, the dotted lines show the position and length of the input fields:

```
Item-no    ----      Description  -----------
Quantity   ----      Cost         ------
```

In the next question, use the following field names and screen positions: SN-ITEM (0220), SN-DESC (0242), SN-QTY (0420) and SN-COST (0442).

◐ Qu 8.11 Assuming the statement ACCEPT SN-REC AT 0101 will accept the above fields, write a record description for SN-REC. (The answer is on page 119).

With CIS COBOL, a special utility program called FORMS-2 is provided to help in producing forms. You layout the form as it will appear on the screen, with labels and input field positions (and types), and FORMS-2 will create the record description.

Ans 8.8 Triple

Ans 8.9 (a) SELECT OUT-FILE ASSIGN TO ":LP:".
       (b) OPEN OUTPUT OUT-FILE.
       (c) WRITE OUT-REC AFTER ADVANCING 1 LINE.
In (c) the entry AFTER ADVANCING 1 LINE can be omitted.

Exercise D

The program below will create the questionnaire data file used in Exercise B (page 77).

A special record has been set up for screen input (SN-REC). The following form is displayed permanently on the screen during the program run:

```
QUESTIONNAIRE INPUT

Reply Y/N/D     ( )
Sex M/F         ( )
Age             ( )
```

The brackets show the position and length of fields. The user can move backwards and forwards between fields using the cursor keys.

Note the first two statements in the IN-DATA paragraph clear the current contents of the fields on the screen, while of course the form itself remains displayed.

A more complete program would check, or *validate*, the input data for errors. For example, sex must be M or F so any other reply should be rejected with an error message. Input validation can often take up a significant part of a program.

We have used the data-name COUNTER rather than COUNT since the latter is a reserved word in some COBOL versions.

Now answer these questions:

(a) Suppose COUNTER contains 008020 and the user types N in reply to the ANOTHER RECORD? prompt. What is then displayed on line 8 of the screen?

(b) Modify the program in Exercise C so that when a new record is added, the record is accepted from the screen as a whole rather than accepting each field separately.

```
ENVIRONMENT DIVISION.
INPUT-OUTPUT SECTION.
FILE-CONTROL.
     SELECT DATA-FILE ASSIGN TO "QUEST.DAT".
```

Ans 8.10   (a) PIC X(2)   (b) PIC X(39)   (c) PIC X(80)   (d) PIC X(279)

```cobol
       DATA DIVISION.
       FILE SECTION.
       FD   DATA-FILE.
       01   DATA-REC.
            02   REPLY      PIC X.
            02   SEX        PIC X.
            02   AGE        PIC 99.
       WORKING-STORAGE SECTION.
       01   SN-REC.
            02   FILLER     PIC X(264).
            02   SN-REPLY   PIC X.
            02   FILLER     PIC X(79).
            02   SN-SEX     PIC X.
            02   FILLER     PIC X(79).
            02   SN-AGE     PIC 99.
       01   COUNTER         PIC 9(6)      VALUE ZERO.
       01   COUNTER-E       PIC Z(5)9.
       01   ANS             PIC X         VALUE SPACE.

       PROCEDURE DIVISION.
            DISPLAY SPACE UPON CRT.
            DISPLAY "QUESTIONNAIRE INPUT" AT 0210.
            DISPLAY "Reply Y/N/D      ( )"   AT 0410.
            DISPLAY "Sex M/F          ( )"   AT 0510.
            DISPLAY "Age              ( )"   AT 0610.
      *process the file
            OPEN OUTPUT DATA-FILE.
            PERFORM IN-DATA UNTIL ANS = "N".
            CLOSE DATA-FILE.
            DISPLAY "Number of records entered" AT 0810.
            MOVE COUNTER TO COUNTER-E.
            DISPLAY COUNTER-E AT 0837.
            STOP RUN.
       IN-DATA.
      *clear screen fields and accept data
            MOVE SPACE TO SN-REC.
            DISPLAY SN-REC AT 0101.          ← clears the fields on the screen
            ACCEPT SN-REC AT 0101.
      *write record to file and increment counter
            MOVE SN-REPLY TO REPLY.
            MOVE SN-SEX TO SEX.
            MOVE SN-AGE TO AGE.
            WRITE DATA-REC.
            ADD 1 TO COUNTER.
            DISPLAY "Another record? Y/N" AT 2010.
            ACCEPT ANS AT 2031.
```

Postscript

This book has discussed the following areas:
processing statements — arithmetic, assignment (MOVE), decision (IF-ELSE), branching (PERFORM), repetition (PERFORM-UNTIL);
screen input-output – ACCEPT and DISPLAY statements, cursor control, edited output, forms layout;
fields and records — numeric and alphanumeric fields, field and record description;
file handling — sequential and random (indexed) files, reading (READ), adding (WRITE), updating (REWRITE), and deleting (DELETE) records.

Several topics have been introduced but not covered in detail: arithmetic and MOVE statements involving different field types or sizes (pages 32 and 43); dynamic access to files, multikey indexed files and relative files (page 88); edited fields (page 99); output to a printer (pages 60 and 100); and data validation (page 104 and the next topic below).

Below, some topics not included in this book are outlined briefly:

Condition forms	Various conditions forms are available for IF statements. We have already mentioned compound conditions (page 22). Another form is NUMERIC, which is used to validate numeric input (including testing for leading zeros in CIS COBOL, provided the field is part of a record and contains spaces before input).
PERFORM options	PERFORM-TIMES and PERFORM-VARYING statements execute a paragraph a pre-set number of times (similar to FOR-NEXT loops in BASIC).
Tables	Tables and lists of similar fields can be set up using an OCCURS option in field descriptions. (Tables are called *arrays* in BASIC.)
REDEFINES CLAUSE	This clause allows the same physical field to be given different field descriptions. This can increase flexibility and save memory space.
Subprograms	A program can call other subprograms (using a CALL statement). The subprograms are separately written and tested, and a library of such programs can be built up. Subprograms have similarities to

procedures that some versions of BASIC provide.

GO TO statements   This statement branches to a specified paragraph. It is equivalent to GOTO statements in BASIC (note the space in the COBOL statement). For reasons given below, GO TO statements are not encouraged, and they can usually be avoided by using the repetition and decision statements described in this book.

The last topic considered here is programming strategy. We have not explicitly referred to strategy up to now for two reasons: first, the COBOL paragraph structure (without GO TO statements) tends to encourage good programming strategy; and second, strategy is more difficult to illustrate with the short programs used in this book than with longer programs.

However, even with the questionnaire program on page 77 you can begin to see the need to organize the program. The ANALYSIS paragraph is related to the initial sequence of statements and itself has two related 'subparagraphs': YES-REPLIES and NO-REPLIES. As this type of breakdown continues, the organization of the program becomes more difficult to follow. One approach is to include prefixes in paragraph names to make the organization clearer. For example, the paragraph names could now be:

    A-ANALYSIS
        A1-YES-REPLIES
        A2-NO-REPLIES
    B-DISPLAY-RESULTS

Various prefix coding systems are used. Hierarchy or organization charts also help to make the hierarchy of the paragraphs clearer.

Good programming strategy starts with *top-down* design. Here a task to be performed by a program is broken down into a series of subtasks (often using a hierarchy chart). These in turn may be broken down further, until a number of self-contained units or modules are identified. These units can then become the paragraphs of the program. To a large extent, top-down design simply formalizes a basic human technique for solving problems by breaking them down into smaller more manageable units.

Structured programming techniques avoid using GO TO statements to jump about in a program; frequent or indiscriminate use of GO TO statements can lead to 'spaghetti' programs with multiple tangled paths that are very difficult to read, understand and correct. GO TO statements can usually be avoided by a full range of repetition statements (like PERFORM-UNTIL and PERFORM-TIMES) and a full decision statement (IF-ELSE); we specify full here since some languages do not provide all these statements, including many versions of BASIC and even some versions of COBOL.

Programming strategy is a vitally important subject and should be studied further by the serious programmer.

There are many comprehensive books on COBOL available that cover the topics mentioned in this Postscript, including:

"COBOL Programming: A structured Approach", P. Abel, Reston, Second Edition 1984.

"A Simplified Guide to Structured COBOL Programming", D. D. McCracken, Wiley 1976.

"COBOL for Micros", N. Stang, Newnes 1983 (which is based on CIS COBOL, but does not explicitly consider programming strategy).

Appendix 1 Layout of a COBOL program

Each line of a COBOL program be be up to 80 characters long, divided as follows:

```
1 2 3 4 5 6 | 7 | 8 9 10 11 | 12 . . .72 | 73 . . .80
              Area A        Area B
```

Columns 8 to 11 form Area A, and columns 12 to 72 form Area B.
Rules for program layout are as follows:

1 Columns 8–11 (Area A). The following entries must start in Area A (at column 8 in this book):
   (a) division headings
   (b) section headings
   (c) paragraph names
   (d) FD in file descriptions
   (e) 01 record level numbers

2 Columns 12–72 (Area B). The following entries must be wholly within Area B:
   (a) SELECT clauses
   (b) filenames in file descriptions
   (c) record and field descriptions (except 01 level numbers)
   (d) statements

3 Columns 1–6. These columns can contain optional sequence numbers to identify lines. We have not normally used sequence numbers in this book to reduce clutter. But they can be useful for debugging.

4 Column 7. This column can contain several characters, including:
   (a) an asterisk to show the line contains a comment (like a REM statement in BASIC)
   (b) a hyphen to show line continuation
   Rules for line continuation and other uses of column 7 can be found in more comprehensive books on COBOL.

5 Columns 73–80. This area is normally blank, but it can be used for comments or program identification.

Appendix 2 Running a COBOL program

COBOL programs contain up to four divisions: Identification, Environment, Data and Procedure Divisions. Some COBOL versions require all four divisions in every program, others do not (see also page 45). For versions that require all four divisions, the following entries may be required in every program:

```
IDENTIFICATION DIVISION.
PROGRAM-ID.   program-name.

ENVIRONMENT DIVISION.
CONFIGURATION SECTION.
SOURCE-COMPUTER.   computer-type.
OBJECT-COMPUTER.   computer-type.
```

although most microcomputer versions require only the heading in the Environment Division. You must supply the program-name and the computer-type (the computer-type will be given in your COBOL reference manual, and the purpose of the computer-type entries is given on page 112). In the program below, we have used the program-name DEMO and a fictitious computer-type ABCD.

Below is a short demonstration program. With CIS COBOL only the Procedure Division is required:

```
IDENTIFICATION DIVISION.
PROGRAM-ID.   DEMO.

ENVIRONMENT DIVISION.
CONFIGURATION SECTION.
SOURCE-COMPUTER.   ABCD.
OBJECT-COMPUTER.   ABCD.

DATA DIVISION.

PROCEDURE DIVISON.
PARAGRAPH.
    DISPLAY "MY FIRST PROGRAM".
    STOP RUN.
```

not needed in all COBOL versions

Some COBOL versions may require single quotes around MY FIRST PROGRAM instead of double quotes in the DISPLAY statement. These quotes have the same effect as quotes in PRINT statements in BASIC. So when the program is run, the following output will be displayed on the screen:

MY FIRST PROGRAM

In this program, most microcomputer versions of COBOL will require only the heading in the Environment Division (like the Data Division), and CIS COBOL requires only the Procedure Division. In fact in CIS COBOL, the PARAGRAPH and STOP RUN entries can also be omitted, so the program becomes:

PROCEDURE DIVISION.
    DISPLAY "MY FIRST PROGRAM".

When typing in your program, start all lines except the DISPLAY and STOP RUN entries at column 8 on the screen (by pressing the space bar eight times). Start the DISPLAY and STOP RUN lines at column 12.

It is very easy to make mistakes when typing in COBOL programs. Be sure to include all full stops and hyphens, and to spell everything correctly. It is a good idea to run a simple program like this one for practice before trying other programs in the book.

If you are anxious to try another program now and have not yet reached Unit 4, you could skim through pages 42 to 44 and then run the program on page 45.

The procedure for running a COBOL program is given after the next section.

Operating systems and compilers

Before we describe how to run a COBOL program, we need to introduce operating systems and compilers.

An *operating system* is the software that controls the internal operations of a computer. CIS COBOL runs under an operating system called CP/M (Control Program Monitor) and can run on computers that provide CP/M (including the BBC microcomputer with a second Z80 processor). CP/M is held on disk and may be loaded automatically when the system is started up, or you may need to type a command such as CPM.

Under CP/M, programs and data are held on disk in named areas called *files* (program files are simlar in principle to data files discussed in Unit 6 except a program file now holds a program rather than data). You supply a file-name when typing in a program, and the program is subsequently identified by that file-name. The format of file-names under CP/M is:

name.extension

where the *name* can contain up to eight characters and the *extension* up to three characters. The extension is used to show the type of file, and is sometimes optional. Earlier in this book we used the extension DAT for a data file, and now we will use the extension CBL for a COBOL program file. Here are two examples of file-names:

    CUST.DAT
    STOCK.CBL

The file called CUST.DAT contains data, and the file called STOCK.CBL contains a COBOL program.

For data files, the CP/M file-name is the external file-name used in the Environment Division (see page 69).

Note: CIS COBOL can also run under the MS-DOS operating system. Procedures are similar.

Now we turn to *compilers*. Internally, a computer does not use symbols such as letters and numbers, but uses a special language or code of its own called *machine language*. A computer must translate a program written in COBOL into machine language before the program can be run. The translation is done by a compiler, and the process is called compilation. The compiler is itself a program and is stored on the disk holding the COBOL system.

The program you write is called the *source* program. The program produced by the compiler is called the *object* program.

Note that the Environment Division on page 110 contains SOURCE-COMPUTER and OBJECT-COMPUTER entries. The source computer compiles the source program, and the object computer runs the object program. Normally the source computer and the object computer are the same.

Developing and running a program

We can now outline the process of developing and running a COBOL program, but you must refer to your COBOL manual (and perhaps a CP/M manual) for details. There are three main stages:

1 *Typing in*   Typing in or amending a program is usually called *editing*. For this stage you need an editor or a word processing package. In CIS COBOL, the program must be saved under a valid CP/M file-name (here we will use the file-name MYFILE.CBL).

2 *Compiling*   When a program has been typed in (or amended), it must be compiled. In CIS COBOL, the command is:

    COBOL MYFILE.CBL

The compiler detects any errors in the program such as undefined fields or missing full stops. If there are any errors, messages are displayed on the screen and the compilation is reported as unsuccessful. You must then return to stage 1 and correct the errors.

3 *Running* If the compilation is successful, the program can be run. In CIS COBOL, the command is:

    RUNA MYFILE.INT

where the extension INT is mandatory. INT stands for intermediate code, which is a form of machine language. MYFILE.INT is the name of the file containing the compiled program.

    Finally, you may be wondering about the process of translating BASIC programs into machine language. BASIC programs are usually translated by an *interpreter* rather than a compiler. An interpreter translates a program statement by statement as it is run. Thus, unlike a compiled program, an interpreted program is translated *every* time it is run. This means programs take longer to run, which becomes significant with larger programs. But an interpreter does cut out the separate translation state, which is more convenient for correcting errors or making amendments.

Summary of COBOL version differences

We have noted several differences between COBOL versions in this book. Listed below are the differences that will prevent some programs in the book running in other versions, and so will require changes to the programs:

- Identification, Environment and Data Division entries may be required in all programs (pages 45 and 110).

- In SELECT clauses, the format for specifying devices may differ (page 69).

- The method of creating indexed files may differ (page 88).

- In file definitions, the LABEL RECORDS clause may be required (page 65).

- All statements may need to be in paragraphs (page 23).

- The statement for clearing the screen may differ (page 33), and DISPLAY statements may need single quotes (page 30).

- The format for specifying the cursor position in ACCEPT and DISPLAY statements may differ (page 36).

- You will find details of these differences in the reference manual for your version of COBOL.

Answers to Further Questions and Exercises

Unit 1

1.14 No full stop after the division heading.
The word TO is not allowed in the ADD statement.

1.15 PROCEDURE DIVISION.
SUBTRACT 200 FROM PAY GIVING TAXABLE.
MULTIPLY TAXABLE BY 0.35 GIVING TAX.
DISPLAY TAX.
STOP RUN.

1.16 PROCEDURE DIVISION.
MOVE 62848 TO OLD.
MOVE 63178 TO NEW.
SUBTRACT OLD FROM NEW GIVING UNITS.
MULTIPLY UNITS BY 4 GIVING CHARGE.
DISPLAY UNITS.
DISPLAY CHARGE.
STOP RUN.

Unit 2

2.15 HIGHER.
ACCEPT C.
ACCEPT D.
IF C > D
    DISPLAY C
ELSE.
    DISPLAY D.

2.16   PROCEDURE DIVISION.
           ACCEPT MARKS-1.
           ACCEPT MARKS-2.
           ACCEPT MARKS-3.
           ADD MARKS-1, MARKS-2, MARKS-3 GIVING TOT-MARKS.
           IF TOT-MARKS NOT < 45 DISPLAY TOT-MARKS.
           STOP RUN.

2.17   All integer numbers between 100 and 250 inclusive.

Unit 3

3.10   Before the PERFORM statement insert the following statements:

           DISPLAY "Type exchange rate".
           ACCEPT EX-RATE.

       Change the MULTIPLY statement to:

           MULTIPLY DOLLARS BY EX-RATE GIVING FRANCS.

3.11   PROCEDURE DIVISION.
           MOVE ZERO TO TOTAL, COUNTER.
           MOVE SPACE TO ANS.
           PERFORM CONVERSION UNTIL ANS = "N".
           DIVIDE COUNTER INTO TOTAL GIVING AVERAGE.
           DISPLAY "Average" AT 0710.
           DISPLAY AVERAGE AT 0719.
           STOP RUN.
       CONVERSION.
           DISPLAY SPACE UPON CRT.
           DISPLAY "Type number of dollars" AT 0110.
           ACCEPT DOLLARS AT 0134.
           MULTIPLY DOLLARS BY 5 GIVING FRANCS.
           DISPLAY "Number of francs" AT 0310.
           DISPLAY FRANCS AT 0328.
           ADD DOLLARS TO TOTAL.
           ADD 1 TO COUNTER.
     *more data?
           DISPLAY "Another conversion? Y/N" AT 0510.
           ACCEPT ANS AT 0535.

Unit 4

4.9   DATA DIVISION.
       WORKING-STORAGE SECTION.
       01   OLD   PIC 9(5).
       01   NEW   PIC 9(5).
       01   UNITS   PIC 9(5).
       01   CHARGE PIC 9(6).

4.10   DATA DIVISION.
       WORKING-STORAGE SECTION.
       01   C   PIC 99.
       01   D   PIC 99.

       PROCEDURE DIVISION.
       HIGHER.
           DISPLAY SPACE UPON CRT.
           ACCEPT C AT 0110.
           ACCEPT D AT 0310.
           IF C > D
               DISPLAY C AT 0510
           ELSE
               DISPLAY D AT 0510.
           STOP RUN.

4.11   DATA DIVISION.
       WORKING-STORAGE SECTION.
       01   NAME   PIC X(20).
       01   NIGHTS   PIC 99.
       01   RATE   PIC 99.
       01   CHARGE   PIC 999.
       01   TOT-NIGHTS PIC 9(5).
       01   TOT-CHARGE PIC 9(6).
       01   ANS   PIC X.

Unit 5

5.10   No hyphen in WORKING-STORAGE.
       No full stop after MILES-REC.

5.11   PROCEDURE DIVISION.
           DISPLAY SPACE UPON CRT.
           ACCEPT MILES-REC AT 0110.
           SUBTRACT INITIAL MILES FROM FINAL MILES GIVING MILES-DRIVEN.
           MULTIPLY MILES-DRIVEN BY 20 GIVING CHARGE.
           DISPLAY CHARGE AT 0310.
           STOP RUN.

5.12   DATA DIVISION.
       WORKING-STORAGE SECTION.
       01   TIME.
             02   HRS   PIC 99.
             02   FILLER   PIC X.
             02   MINS   PIC 99.
       01   STORE   PIC 9(4).

       PROCEDURE DIVISION.
           DISPLAY SPACE UPON CRT.
           ACCEPT TIME AT 0110.
           MULTIPLY HRS BY 60 GIVING STORE.
           ADD MINS TO STORE.
           DISPLAY STORE AT 0310.
           STOP RUN.

Unit 6

6.11   ENVIRONMENT DIVISION.
       INPUT-OUTPUT SECTION.
       FILE-CONTROL.
           SELECT CUSTOMER-FILE ASSIGN TO "CUST.DAT".

       DATA DIVISION.
       FILE SECTION.
       FD   CUSTOMER-FILE.
       01   CUSTOMER-RECORD.
             02   NAME   PIC X(20).
             02   ADDRESS
                   03   STREET   PIC X(20).
                   03   TOWN   PIC X(20).
                   03   POST-CODE   PIC X(8).
             02   ORDER-VALUE   PIC 9(6).
       WORKING-STORAGE SECTION.
       01   EOF   PIC X   VALUE SPACE.

6.12 PROCEDURE DIVISION.
        OPEN INPUT CUSTOMER-FILE.
        READ CUSTOMER-FILE AT END MOVE "E" TO EOF.
        PERFORM TOWN-TEST UNTIL EOF = "E".
        CLOSE CUSTOMER-FILE.
        STOP RUN.
TOWN-TEST.
        IF TOWN = "BRIGHTON" DISPLAY NAME.
        READ CUSTOMER-FILE AT END MOVE "E" TO EOF.

Unit 7

7.10 ENVIRONMENT DIVISION.
INPUT-OUTPUT SECTION.
FILE-CONTROL.
        SELECT CAR-FILE ASSIGN TO "CAR.DAT"
            ORGANIZATION IS INDEXED
            ACCESS IS RANDOM
            RECORD KEY IS REG-NO.

DATA DIVISION.
FILE SECTION.
FD CAR-FILE.
01 CAR-REC.
    02   REG-NO   PIC X(7).
    02   OWNER   PIC X(20).
WORKING-STORAGE SECTION.
01 FLAG   PIC X   VALUE "S".

7.11 INQUIRY.
        MOVE SPACE TO REG-NO.
        DISPLAY "Type registration number".
        ACCEPT REG-NO.
        READ CAR-FILE INVALID KEY MOVE "U" TO FLAG.
        IF FLAG = "U"
            DISPLAY "No such record"
        ELSE
            DISPLAY "Owner ", OWNER.

7.12 ADDITION.
    MOVE SPACE TO REG-NO, OWNER.
    DISPLAY "Type registration number".
    ACCEPT REG-NO.
    DISPLAY "Type owner".
    ACCEPT OWNER.
    WRITE CAR-REC INVALID KEY
        DISPLAY "Duplicate registration number".

Unit 8

8.7 DATA DIVISION.
WORKING-STORAGE SECTION.
01   NUM   PIC 9(4)V99.
01   NUM-E PIC ZZZ9.99.
01   ANS   PIC X VALUE SPACE.

PROCEDURE DIVISION.
    PERFORM DEMO UNTIL ANS = "N".
    STOP RUN.
DEMO.
    DISPLAY SPACE UPON CRT.
    MOVE ZERO TO NUM.
    ACCEPT NUM AT 0110.
    ADD 8 TO NUM.
    MOVE NUM TO NUM-E.
    DISPLAY NUM-E AT 0310.
    DISPLAY "Another number?" AT 0510.
    ACCEPT ANS AT 0527.

8.11 01   SN-REC.
       02   FILLER   PIC X(99).
       02   SN-ITEM   PIC X(4).
       02   FILLER   PIC X(18).
       02   SN-DESC   PIC X(10).
       02   FILLER   PIC X(128).
       02   SN-QTY   PIC 9(4).
       02   FILLER   PIC X(18).
       02   SN-COST   PIC 9(6).

Exercise A

A-1 (a) Charge 88
    (b) Charge 60

A-2 PROCEDURE DIVISION.
         MOVE SPACE TO ANS.
         MOVE ZERO TO TOT-NIGHTS, TOT-CHARGE.
         PERFORM COSTS UNTIL ANS = "N".
         DISPLAY "Total nights" AT 0510.
         DISPLAY TOT-NIGHTS AT 0524.
         DISPLAY "Total charge" AT 0710.
         DISPLAY TOT-CHARGE AT 0724.
         STOP RUN.
     COSTS.
         DISPLAY SPACE UPON CRT.
         DISPLAY "Type number of nights" AT 0110.
         ACCEPT NIGHTS AT 0133.
         IF NIGHTS = 1
             MOVE 15 TO RATE
         ELSE
             IF NIGHTS NOT > 7
                 MOVE 12 TO RATE
             ELSE IF NIGHTS NOT > 28
                     MOVE 10 TO RATE
                 ELSE
                     MOVE 7 TO RATE.
         MULTIPLY NIGHTS BY RATE GIVING CHARGE.
         DISPLAY "Charge" AT 0310.
         DISPLAY CHARGE AT 0318.
         ADD NIGHTS TO TOT-NIGHTS.
         ADD CHARGE TO TOT-CHARGE.
    *more data?
         DISPLAY "Another bill? Y/N" AT 1210.
         ACCEPT ANS AT 1229.

A-3 PROCEDURE DIVISION.
          DISPLAY SPACE UPON CRT.
          DISPLAY "Type number of hours" AT 0110.
          ACCEPT HRS AT 0129.
          IF HRS NOT > 40
              MULTIPLY HRS BY 2 GIVING PAY
          ELSE
              IF HRS NOT > 50
                  SUBTRACT 40 FROM HRS
                  MULTIPLY HRS BY 3 GIVING HIGH-PAY
                  ADD 80, HIGH-PAY GIVING PAY
              ELSE
                  SUBTRACT 50 FROM PAY
                  MULTIPLY HRS BY 4 GIVING HIGH-PAY
                  ADD 80, 30, HIGH-PAY GIVING PAY.
          DISPLAY "Pay" AT 0310.
          DISPLAY PAY AT 0315.
          STOP RUN.

Exercise B

(a) Total answering Yes   1552
    Total answering No   1262

    Total of males answering Yes   0737
    Total over age 40 answering Yes 1171

(b) Insert in the Working-Storage Section:

    02   NO-UN-25   PIC 9(4)   VALUE ZERO.

    Add to the NO-REPLIES paragraph:
         IF AGE < 25 ADD 1 TO NO-UN-25.

    Add to the DISPLAY-RESULTS paragraph:
         DISPLAY "Total under age 25 answering No" AT 0610.
         DISPLAY NO-UN-25 AT 0643.

(c) Insert in the Working-Storage Section:

    02   TOT-REPLIES   PIC 9(5)   VALUE ZERO.

Insert in the ANALYSIS paragraph *before* the READ statement:

    ADD 1 TO TOT-REPLIES.

Insert in the DISPLAY-RESULTS paragraph:

    DISPLAY "Total answering the question" AT 0710.
    DISPLAY TOT-REPLIES AT 0743.

Exercise C

(a) 1 Duplicate membership number
     2 nothing
     3 Member paid   Y
     4 No such record
     5 nothing
     6 No such record

(b) UPDATE.
    DISPLAY SPACE UPON CRT.
    DISPLAY "Type membership number for update" AT 0110.
    ACCEPT MEM-NO AT 0145.
    READ MEMBERS INVALID KEY MOVE "U" TO FLAG.
    IF FLAG = "U"
        DISPLAY "No such record" AT 0310
    ELSE
        DISPLAY "Has member paid? Y/N" AT 0310
        ACCEPT STATUS AT 0332
        REWRITE MEM-REC INVALID KEY DISPLAY "Error" AT 0510.
    DISPLAY "Press RETURN to continue" AT 1210.
    ACCEPT ANS AT 1236.

Exercise D

(a) Number of records entered △△△△8020

(The number 8020 starts at position 39 on line 8 because of two spaces replacing the leading zeros)

(b) Insert in the Working-Storage Section:

```
01  SN-REC.
    02  FILLER      PIC X(46).
    02  SN-MEM-NO   PIC X(4).
    02  FILLER      PIC X(141).
    02  SN-STATUS   PIC X.
```

In the ADDITION paragraph, delete the first ACCEPT statement and replace the second ACCEPT statement by:

```
MOVE SPACE TO SN-REC.
ACCEPT SN-REC AT 0101.
MOVE SN-MEM-NO TO MEM-NO.
MOVE SN-STATUS TO STATUS.
```

Index

ACCEPT statements, 18, 46
  format, 18, 36
ACCESS entry, 78, 86–8
  format, 86
Accessing records, 78, 79
ADD statements, 3, 10
  formats, 14, 25
Adding records, 82
Alphanumeric
  fields, 31–3, 59
  literals, 30, 32
Alphabetic fields, 32
AND, in conditions, 22
Area A and B, 15, 109
Arithmetic statements, 5
  formats, 14, 25
Arrays, in BASIC, 106
Assignment statements, 8
AT option, 36–7, 80

BASIC, 2–4
  (each BASIC topic has a separate entry in the index, e.g. Arrays)
BBC microcomputer, 111
Blanks, in numbers, 99

CIS COBOL, 2
  summary of version differences, 113
CLOSE statements, 66, 73
COBOL, 2
  summary of version differences, 113
COBOL command, 113
Columns, on screen, 109
Compilation, 112
Compiler, 112
Commas, in numbers, 99
  in programs, 5, 14
Comments, in programs, 34
Compound conditions, 8
Condition forms, 19, 106
  compound, 22
  NUMERIC, 106
Configuration Section, 110
CP/M, 111
CRT, 33
Currency signs, 99
Cursor control keys, 57–8
Cursor position, 36–7

Data-names, 11
Data Division, 42, 45, 110
DATA statements, in BASIC, 68
DB (debit), 99
Decimal numbers, 94–5
  output of, 97
DELETE statements, 84
Deleting records, 84
Disk files, 64
DISPLAY statements, 6, 30, 36
  formats, 14, 36
DIVIDE statements, 5
  formats, 14, 25
Divisions, COBOL, 4, 45, 110
  headings, 5, 109
DYNAMIC access, 86, 88

Edited fields, 96–9
  and arithmetic, 98
Editing a program, 112
Ellipsis, 13
ELSE option, 19
END, in READ statements, 66, 87

Environment Division, 45, 68, 110
Extension, in CP/M file-names, 111–2
External file-names, 69, 111

FD entry, 64
Field descriptions, 42–3
  format, 62
Fields, 7, 9
  elementary, 54
  group, 54, 55, 59
  receiving, 8, 9
  sending, 8, 9
  size of, 42, 43
  see also, Alphanumeric, Numeric
Figurative constants/literals, 33
FILE-CONTROL paragraph, 69
File-names, 64
  external, 69, 111
  internal, 69
File descriptions, 64, 65
File Section, 65, 67–8
  and VALUE clauses, 61
Files, 64
  see also, Indexed, Program, Random and Sequential files
FILLER fields, 56–8, 100, 102
Floating signs, 99
Formats, general, 12–13
Forms, 102–103, 104
FORMS-2, 103
FOR-NEXT statement, in BASIC, 106
Full stops, in
  divisions, 5
  field descriptions, 44
  file descriptions, 65
  paragraphs, 23
  SELECT clauses, 69, 79
  statements, 5
  IF, 20
  READ, 74

General formats, rules for, 12–3
GIVING option, 25
GO TO statements, 107

Hierarchy charts, 107

Identification Division, 45, 110
Identifiers, 14
IF statements, 19–22
  format, 28
Imperative statements, 66
Indexed files, 78
  accessing records, 79–80
  adding records, 82
  creating, 88
  deleting records, 84
  multikey, 88
  sequential access to, 86–88
  vs. sequential files, 87
  updating records, 83
Initialization of fields, 33, 34, 35
INPUT statements, in BASIC, 18
Input-Output Section, 69
Internal file-name, 69
Interpreters, in BASIC, 113
INVALID KEY entry,
  in DELETE, 84
  in READ, 79, 86
  in REWRITE, 83
  in WRITE, 82, 86
I-O option, 73, 83, 84

Key fields, 79
  duplicate, 82, 88

LABEL RECORDS entry, 65
Layout, program, 15, 109
Leading zeros, see Zeros
Level numbers, 42, 53, 54
Line continuation, 109
Literals, 11, 30
  figurative, 33
  non-numeric, 31
  see also Numeric, Alphanumeric

Machine language, 112
Menus, 85, 92
Microfocus, 2
Modules, 107
MOVE statements, 8, 10, 49
  and field size, 43
  and field type, 32, 33
  format, 14
MS-DOS, 112
MULTIPLY statements, 5
  formats, 14, 25

Negative numbers,
  input of, 95
  output of, 99
Non-numeric literals, 31
NUMERIC, condition form, 106
Numeric fields, 31
  decimal, 94–5
  edited, 96–9
  and MOVE statements, 32, 33
  signed, 95
Numeric literals, 30, 31
  and MOVE statements, 32, 33

Object
  computer, 110, 112
  program, 112
OCCURS clause, 106
OPEN statements, 72–3
  EXTEND, 73
  format, 72
  INPUT, 67, 80
  I-O, 73, 83, 84
  OUTPUT, 71, 82, 88, 101
Operating systems, 111
OR, in conditions, 22
ORGANIZATION entry, 78, 86, 88
  format, 86

Paragraphs, 23
Paper tape, 64
PERFORM statements, 24, 26–7, 106
  condition testing, 70
PIC, 42
PICTURE clauses, 42–3
  decimal, 94
  edited, 96–9
  signed, 95
PRINT statements, in BASIC, 7
Program files, 111
Programming strategy, 107

Quotes, in DISPLAY statements, 30
  in BASIC, 30

Random files, 78, 88
READ statements
  full stop in, 74
  in BASIC, 68

  in indexed files, 79, 87
  in sequential files, 66
Record descriptions, 52–5
RECORD KEY entry, 79
  format, 86
Records, 52
  and screen input, 57–9, 102–3
  and screen output, 56
REM statements, in BASIC, 34
Repetition statements, 106, 107
Reserved words, 11
  examples, 55, 76, 104
REWRITE statement
  in indexed files, 83
  in sequential files, 84
ROUNDED option, 14
RUNA command, 113
Running programs, 2, 46, 112–3

Screen
  clearing, 33, 37, 91
  input, 47–9, 57–9, 102–3
  layout, 37
  output, 48, 56
SELECT clause, 68–9, 78–9
  format, 86, 89
Sequential files, 64, 78
  input and output, Unit 6
  vs. indexed files, 87
  updating, 84
Signed fields, 95
Source
  computer, 110, 112
  program, 112
SPACE, 33, 49
Statements, 4–5
STOP RUN, 7
Structured programs, 76, 107
Subprograms, 106
SUBTRACT statements, 5
  formats, 14, 25

Tables, 106
Tape, 64, 79
Text, 30
Top-down design, 107
Totals, 35
Transaction files, 84
Translation, program, 112–3

UNTIL option, 27
Updating
  indexed files, 83
  sequential files, 84

Validation, data, 104, 106
VALUE clauses, 60–1
Variables, 7

Working-Storage Section, 44, 67–8
  and VALUE clauses, 61
WRITE statement
  in indexed files, 82, 87
  in sequential files, 71
  in print files, 100–1

ZERO, 33, 71
Zeros, leading
  input of, 47
  output of, 48
  suppression on output, 96, 99
  validation on input, 106